D0151933

Musical Thought in Britain and Germany During the Early Eighteenth Century

American University Studies

Series V
Philosophy

Vol. 26

PETER LANG
New York · Bern · Frankfurt am Main · Paris

Donald R. Boomgaarden

Musical Thought in Britain and Germany During the Early Eighteenth Century

PETER LANG
New York · Bern · Frankfurt am Main · Paris

Library of Congress Cataloging-in-Publication Data

Boomgaarden, Donald R.
Musical thought in Britain and Germany during the early eighteenth century.

(American university studies. Series V, Philosophy; vol. 26)
Bibliography: p.
Includes index.
1. Music—Great Britain—18th century—History and criticism. 2. Music—Germany—18th century—History and criticism. 3. Music—Great Britain—18th century—Philosophy and aesthetics. 4. Music—Germany—18th century—Philosophy and aesthetics. I. Title. II. Series: American university studies. Series V, Philosophy; v. 26.
ML195.B66 1987 780'.941 86-27658
ISBN 0-8204-0391-1
ISSN 0739-6392

CIP-Kurztitelaufnahme der Deutschen Bibliothek

Boomgaarden, Donald R.:
Musical thought in Britain and Germany during the early eighteenth century / Donald R. Boomgaarden. – New York; Bern; Frankfurt am Main; Paris: Lang, 1987.
(American University Studies: Ser. 5, Philosophy; Vol. 26)
ISBN 0-8204-0391-1

NE: American University Studies / 05

Printed by Weihert-Druck GmbH, Darmstadt, West Germany

TO BARBARA

TABLE OF CONTENTS

CHAPTER I

INTRODUCTION

Issues in Eighteenth-Century Musical Thought

This study examines the musical thought of the eighteenth century from a vantage point different from that taken by most historians up to now, emphasizing musical events and concepts in Britain and Germany, along with the cross-fertilization of ideas which took place between those two countries. While no one can deny the great importance of France in the development of musical thought, British and German intellectual circles never blindly assimilated French ideas. French neoclassicism is not the same as British neoclassicism, and German neoclassicism is something different from both. The authors of the German *Aufklärung* and the British Enlightenment each sought to create a unique national art, achieved not through slavish imitation of French models, but by creating viable alternatives.

There were, of course, differences between British and German musical thought during the century. This was partly a result of the fact that German writers were usually practicing musicians, whereas British aestheticians were often men of letters. Still, the similarities between the two are great enough that, even if there were no evidence at all, one would have to suspect some type of contact between the writers on music in both nations. That there is evidence that has not been brought together in any systematic fashion is one of the primary reasons for this study.

But what of British and German musical thought itself? While some aspects of eighteenth-century German and British attitudes toward music have been examined by musicologists in detail (the activity of German musicians in London, for example), current scholarship continues to perpetuate misconceptions. When one reads of the 'classical' period in music, the usual credit for creating the philosophical basis for the movement goes to the French. In F. E. Sparrshot's survey of eighteenth-century musical aesthetics in the New Grove's Dictionary, one is struck by the exclusion of British writers and the mere passing mention of G. E. Lessing, J. G. Herder, and Kant.[1] The remainder of the article deals solely with French authors. Other recent literature does little to correct this situation. Georgia Cowart's recently published dissertation on the origins of music criticism touches upon some of the important issues but in the main focuses on French thought and its influence in Britain and Germany.[2] Bellamy Hosler's monograph on musical aesthetics in eighteenth-century Germany is limited to one particular aspect--instrumental music--and does not take British influences on German musicians into account.[3] Even the admirable recent collection of essays on Johann Mattheson edited by Hans Joachim Marx and George Buelow fails to address the issue of British influence on German musical thought.[4] In her review of the volume Cowart correctly observes that though Herbert Schneider's essay on Mattheson and French music provides an excellent companion to Arno Forchert's earlier examination of French writers and Mattheson, it also "points up the need for similar studies treating the important influence of English culture and thought on Mattheson's writings."[5]

In fact, outside of the pioneering efforts of Walter Serauky, Hugo Goldschmidt, and--more recently--Karl-Heinz Darenberg, British and German thought on music in the first half of the eighteenth century remains largely unexplored.[6] But even these works present problems. Goldschmidt's 1915 study takes an approach which attempts to reconcile eighteenth-century musical thought with that of the romantic era. Serauky's fine work is guided by its rather evolutionary bias, cataloguing attitudes toward only one aesthetic concept (imitation) and attributing too much importance to the work of French writers. Darenberg avoids these pitfalls, but his study is meant as a survey of writers in Britain and does not presume to probe deeply into any important issues.

Aside from the recognition of this situation, the historian is confronted with the complex nature of eighteenth-century German and British musical thought itself. The quantity and quality of material from Enlightenment writers presents us with an embarrassment of riches, and a serious dilemma: how can we do justice to such an enormous quantity of information, and best present the personalities and ideas so critical to our understanding of the age? A diversified approach to the problem seemed necessary. Thus, there are four levels of organization in this study: national (the comparison of

British and German musical thought), individual (the examination of the careers and works of the important writers on music from 1700 to 1740), topical (an in-depth discussion of four important concepts of the period, as viewed by the writers themselves), and chronological (a decade by decade discussion of the trends in these concepts).

For the sake of large-scale organization the first two of these levels, national and individual, are combined in chapters two and three. After a brief discussion of the origins of eighteenth-century musical thought, important personalities who helped shape ideas on music in Britain and Germany--Joseph Addison and Christian Wolff--are examined. Chapter three presents biographies of British and German writers whose works form the basis of this study. Significant interrelationships between the writers of each nation are commented on, as well as certain particularly revealing attitudes toward a number of issues in music theory and aesthetics. For the most part, though, the writers' ideas are reserved for chapters 4, 5, 6, and 7. Each of these chapters is devoted to a systematic examination of eighteenth-century attitudes toward one of the major aesthetic issues of the day: the affections, imitation (or Aristotelian _mimesis_), taste, and imagination. An essentially chronological structure, documenting gradual shifts in these attitudes, prevails within these topical chapters. Although this method of organization seemed the most logical, it should be stressed that all four of these levels of organization are essential, and their combination or separation should not be interpreted as a statement of the relative importance of each.

Four Aesthetic Issues Of The Early Eighteenth Century

One of the essential truths of early eighteenth-century British and German writings on music is that authors often espoused remarkably outdated views in one paragraph only to propose startlingly progressive ones in the next. Any attempt to regard the period as some kind of *Übergangszeit* for concepts which became prevalent later in the century is doomed to failure. Developments in eighteenth-century musical thought never marched irresistibly forward, but often turned to the side, or even about-face. Indeed, some writers marched to an altogether different drummer. But how is it possible to present the aesthetic views of authors who themselves never attempted to write systematically about the arts? Arthur Lovejoy provided one method more than fifty years ago when he examined eighteenth-century attitudes toward one word (in his case "nature") and catalogued the numerous meanings.[7] Frederick Wessel approached this problem in like manner in his study of the affections, choosing to examine the musical presentation of one specific affection throughout the various writings of the period.[8] Although intended to be somewhat broader in purpose, my study follows a similar route, selecting four of the important concepts found in early eighteenth-century writings on music: the affections, imitation, taste, and theories of imagination. On the most basic level it seemed appropriate to choose these terms since, as will be shown, each figures so prominently in writings of the period. The selection of these issues made a comparison of the thought of journalists, philosophers, and musicians possible, since all four concepts were discussed by members of each group (though not with equal emphasis, nor were all discussed by every individual writer). This provided a more comprehensive view than usual of early eighteenth-century musical thought as well as an opportunity to demonstrate that none of these writers lived in an intellectual vacuum. Another, though less significant, reason for choosing these terms was the importance assigned to each by many modern historians, from Hugo Goldschmidt to Gloria Flaherty.

By selecting these terms and presenting them as they appear in the most important writings of the day, it is hoped that these eighteenth-century concepts will be better understood. Structured chronologically, these chapters may better enable the modern reader to appreciate shifts in eighteenth-century attitudes toward these terms through the first four decades of the century. During this period important changes in the perceptions of these concepts did occur. The affections, imitation, and taste all declined in importance. Attitudes toward the concept of the imagination, fueled by the writings of British figures like Addison, became more important, especially in Germany. Ultimately, our modern preconceptions toward what these terms meant to eighteenth-century readers must be reevaluated. To read eighteenth-century treatises on music and not be aware of the meanings these terms had for the readers of that time is, as Lovejoy put it, "to move about in the midst of ambiguities unrealized."[9]

Eighteenth-Century Writers on Music: Criteria For Selection

Choosing the writers to be discussed was no easy task, since one must consider not only writers of musical treatises, but literary men and philosophers as well. Authors of musical treatises were given priority, however, since their works usually deal most directly with musical thought. For this reason almost every music theorist of note in Germany or Britain active between 1700 and 1740 is discussed in this study. One writer, the brilliant Johann Mattheson, stands above all others. His works span the entire period under consideration, and the refinements in his own attitudes over three decades offer the historian important insights into which ideas were more current and which less so. Thus, his early, middle, and late views on each of the terms selected for study are presented in correct chronological context in the chapters devoted to them. Other major figures, like Alexander Malcolm, Johann David Heinichen, Friedrich Lampe, Johann Adolph Scheibe, and Lorenz Mizler, must of course be considered, but also lesser-known writers such as Ernst Gottlieb Baron and Roger North, both of whose comments on aesthetic matters are most valuable.

Eighteenth-century literary figures had a tremendous impact on aesthetic thought, musical or otherwise. For this reason Joseph Addison is included in this study. His *Tatler* and *Spectator* essays, themselves manifestations of the rise of British journalism, contain numerous comments about music, within and beyond the context of the four concepts examined in this study. In Germany, Johann Christoph

Gottsched exerted a considerable influence on musical writers, notably Scheibe and Mizler. For good or ill, literary men had much to say about music. To ignore their thoughts would do violence to any attempt at a perspective of eighteenth-century musical thought.

As for the philosophers, although their influence was not as strong as it had been in the previous century, at least one, Johann Christian Wolff, did exert a powerful and direct impact on several German musicians, including Baron and Mizler. Most importantly, it is in the realm of philosophical thought, especially in the context of the conflict between the empiricism of John Locke and the rise of German rationalism under Wolff, that the works of early eighteenth-century writers on music must be seen. It is true that Locke never commented extensively about music, but his attitudes toward the basic issue of sense perception did have an impact on musical writers in Britain and Germany. Shaftesbury should also be mentioned in this regard, and the work of his student, Francis Hutcheson. For this reason, Hutcheson's important discussions of music also will be examined in this study. A survey of the combined thought of these three groups--musicians, literary men, and philosophers--should provide sufficient basis for any discussion of early eighteenth-century musical thought.

1 F. E. Sparrshot, "Aesthetics," in New Grove's Dictionary, I, 126-127.

2 Georgia Cowart, The Origins of Modern Musical Criticism: French and Italian Music 1600-1750 (Ann Arbor: UMI Research Press, 1981).

3 Bellamy Hosler, Changing Aesthetic Views of Instrumental Music in 18th-Century Germany (Ann Arbor: UMI Research Press, 1981).

4 George J. Buelow and Hans Joachim Marx, eds., New Mattheson Studies (Cambridge: Cambridge University Press, 1983).

5 Georgia Cowart, review of New Mattheson Studies in Musical Quarterly, lxxi (1985), 98-101; See Hermann Schneider, "Mattheson und die französische Musik," in New Mattheson Studies, 425-442. Arno Forchert's study "Französische Autoren in den Schriften Johann Matthesons," can be found in Festschrift Heinz Becker (Laaber: Laaber Verlag, 1982), 382-391.

6 Walter Serauky, Die musikalische Nachahmungsästhetik im Zeitraum von 1700 bis 1850 (Münster: Helios, 1929); Hugo Goldschmidt, Die Musikästhetik des 18. Jahrhunderts (Zurich and Leipzig: Rascher, 1915); Karl-Heinz Darenberg, Studien zur englischen Musikaesthetik des 18. Jahrhunderts. (Hamburg: Cram-de Gruyter, 1960).

7 Arthur O. Lovejoy, "'Nature' as Aesthetic Norm," in Essays in the History of Ideas (Baltimore: Johns Hopkins Press, 1948), 69-77.

8 Frederick Wessel, "The Affektenlehre in the Eighteenth Century" (Ph.D. dissertation, Indiana University, 1967).

9 Lovejoy, "'Nature'," 69.

CHAPTER II

SEVENTEENTH-CENTURY ORIGINS AND EIGHTEENTH-CENTURY TRENDS

The State of Musicography ca. 1700

Britain and Germany shared similar burdens in the seventeenth century: religious strife and bitter civil war. By the middle of the century musical life in both countries had been deeply affected and traditional forms of patronage radically altered. It was in their recovery from these disasters, however, that the two nations differed--a difference which had implications for eighteenth-century developments in musical thought. In Britain the forces of religious radicalism fueled strong prejudices against music. Even though there were occasional bright spots, such as the original approaches to solmization by William Bathe, the single-clef concepts of Thomas Salmon, or the remarkably far-sighted proposal by Lord Brounker for a system of equal temperament based on calculation using logarithms, developments in British musical thought were for the most part adversely affected by the Puritans.[1] This, combined with the destruction of common forms of musical employment, contributed to a marked decline in the quantity of writings on music. Puritan forces banned public performances of music, and writings critical of music in religious celebrations were common.[2] Though Percy Scholes has argued persuasively that it was not so much the music itself as its ornate use in the service that the Puritans rejected, to accept music only as background noise for state occasions reflects a profound lack of appreciation for the art.[3] This situation also contributed to the decline of the native opera tradition and, indirectly, made dependence upon foreign musicians and music an inevitability.

In contrast, German musicians were openly supported by many religious figures and, as economic conditions improved over the century, were able to maintain and enrich their tradition of writing about music. Philosophers like Johannes Kepler (1571-1630) and Gottfried Wilhelm Leibniz (1646-1716) also contributed to the growing literature on music. Kepler's attempt to synthesize religion, metaphysics, science, and art into one whole led the scholar Max Kepler to call him the "German Pythagoras."[4] Even the greatest German novelist of the age, Hans Christoffel von Grimmelshausen (1622-1676) wrote several "musician novels" as did actual musicians like W. C. Printz (1641-1717) and Johann Kuhnau (1660-1722).[5] Johann Beer (1655-1700), who worked as an organist at several Saxon courts, not only wrote an imitation of Grimmelshausen, _Jucundus Jucundissimus_ (1680), but had considerable impact on Johann Mattheson, who included Beer in his _Ehrenpforte_ of 1740.[6] The interest shown by seventeeth-century German literary figures in music, and the literary talent of many musicians, helped to make the works of Mattheson, J. A.

Scheibe, and Lorenz Mizler possible.

Two other important trends--one German and one British--contributed to the great increase in writings on music in the first decades of the eighteenth century. In Germany a new intellectual spirit of some power emerged, a rationalistic philosophy articulated by Christian Wolff. This same period saw the emergence of Joseph Addison as the most influentual literary figure of his age. The success of Addison's *Spectator Papers*, not only in Britain but throughout Europe, was one of the seminal cultural events of the early eighteenth-century. The impact of his writings, and those of Wolff, on the musical writers of the early eighteenth century cannot be overestimated.

Joseph Addison and the Rise of British Journalism

Although journalism began in Britain during the early seventeenth century, the periodical essay so popular in the eighteenth originated somewhat later.[7] It was not until writers of ability, such as John Dryden, contributed to *The Athenian Mercury* (1690-1697) that this unique genre was born, and with it the modern art of criticism.[8] Written to inform *and* entertain, these pamphlets and periodicals featured a light, witty style which became popular throughout Europe. Journalism in Enlightenment Britain did not just focus on artistic criticism, however. Londoners witnessed a number of "paper wars" during the early years of the eighteenth century, wars waged by various individuals for political ends.[9] Though no lives were lost in these Whig and Tory battles, many a career began or ended in the pages of a London pamphlet. Undoubtedly the most famous participants in these bloodless conflicts were

Richard Steele and Joseph Addison. Steele's political interests so dominated his essays that Jonathan Swift dryly commented in 1713: "Mr. Steele is the Author of two tolerable Plays, (or at least of the greatest part of them) which, added to the Company he kept, and to the continual Conversation and Friendship of Mr. Addison, hath given him the Character of a Wit." [10] Because Addison's essays rose above mundane political concerns, Swift judged his writings as the more significant--an evaluation which has stood the test of time. It is in Addison's essays, not Steele's, that one can find the most valuable comments on aesthetic matters.

Joseph Addison's essays in the Tatler and Spectator were famous in their day.[11] The Tatler, which ran from the Spring of 1709 until January of 1711 and had 271 numbers, contained forty-nine issues written wholly by Addison and another twenty-two for which he was at least partially responsible.[12] Thus, of the total numbers issued Addison was actively involved in about one-fifth of them. Addison's share in the 555 issues of the Spectator was much larger, amounting to approximately half. The circulation of the Spectator reached a high point of around 3,000 copies, with a possible five or six readers per copy.[13] Unlike the Tatler, which ran three days a week, the Spectator ran six days a week from March 1, 1711 until December 6, 1712. Between them, the two periodicals spawned some 121 British and Continental imitations including the Female Tatler, the Tatling Harlot, and at least sixteen in the German-speaking countries.[14]

If Addison was a famous man in his own century, his reputation has fallen in ours. The writer whom Benjamin Franklin once encouraged his students to emulate is now regarded with considerable distaste.[15] The late C. S. Lewis commented that "if he is not at present the most hated of our writers, that can only be because he is so little read."[16] Margaret Laurie's entry on Addison in the most recent edition of Grove's reflects, if not antipathy, at least ignorance.[17] After mentioning a few particulars of Addison's life, Laurie informs the reader that he also wrote "several critical essays on opera."[18] Even worse than this type of neglect, however, is the manner in which Addison is misrepresented in recent musicological writings. When he is discussed, particularly his views on opera, a one-dimensional portrait is painted. Siegmund Betz (whose article has served as a basis for most recent writings on Addison and music) made the following comments:

> The operatic criticism of the Tatler and Spectator is almost as much a problem in political thought as it is in literature and musicology. Like the literary and dramatic criticism of the papers, it does not present much that is new in doctrine, but rather crystallizes a set of judgements current among the wits of Queen Anne's day. There is, however, a striking difference in the case of operatic criticism. Steele and Addison, like many other 18th-century men of letters, had only a slight feeling for music. 19

While one can agree with much of Betz's assessment, his opinion about Addison's "slight feeling for music" seems harsh. Even more questionable are Gloria Flaherty's comments, in particular that Addison did not regard opera as important.[20] Addison's libretto for Thomas Clayton's Rosamond, though not excellent, would tend to refute the claims of Betz and Flaherty, and a careful examination of Addison's periodical output fails to reveal the atti- tudes many writers have ascribed to him. On the contrary, as we shall see in later chapters, Addison was capable of writing expressively, eloquently and admiringly about music.

Christian Wolff and German Rationalistic Philosophy

Although Germany had no circle of literary wits of the caliber of Addison or Steele, an upsurge of philosophical and critical activity is one of the hallmarks of the early *Aufklärung*. Yet the German Enlightenment was rather different from that in Britain, where there was also a great increase in scientific activity, and perhaps related to this, the popularity of deism.[21] British scientific advances had little impact in Germany, and religious impulses were if anything, more intense, not less so. And while Britons showed considerable interest in representative forms of government and the natural rights of man, German governmental institutions used the Enlightenment to justify their existence and solidify their position. The anti-establishment forces so powerful in Britain and France, often led by men of high social standing (e.g., Lord Shaftesbury) were less successful in the highly decentralized and economically weak states of Germany. As Lewis White Beck has commented, "Who was to carry the burden of the Enlightenment? A few university professors, who might be silenced or dismissed; a few pastors, who made sure that their best works were published posthumously; here and there there was a misfit without followers."[22] Even Frederick the Great, who may have enjoyed the writings of Voltaire and the scepticism of Locke, never abandoned his royal dictate: "Argue as much as you will, only obey!"[23]

It was into this atmosphere that Christian Wolff (1679-1754), the foremost German philosopher of his age, was born. His writings are of importance to this study for at least three reasons. First, because Wolff had an important influence on several writers on music. Second, because he presents us with the philosophical attitudes most current in the German-speaking world of that time. Third, because there are elements of Wolff's thoughts which are indebted to British writers. If the most important influences upon Hutcheson were Shaftesbury and Locke, the greatest influences on Wolff were Leibniz and Locke. In his study of the influence of British philosophers on German philosophy, G. Zart makes special reference to the influence Locke and Bacon had upon Wolff.[24] The central figure in German philosophy in the 1720s, Christian Wolff exerted an influence upon the university students of northern Germany of surprising magnitude. Joachim Birke, evidently the only scholar who has realized the extent of Wolff's importance in the field of music, pointed out that "the majority of the academic youth celebrated Wolff as the liberator of the spirit from the slavery and inherited musty dogmatism and scholasticism" of the previous century.[25]

The story of Wolff's expulsion from the University of Halle provides an introduction to his philosophy. In 1721 Wolff, upon giving up his post as rector, gave an address entitled "On the Practical Philosophy of the Chinese."[26] By attempting to show that human happiness was possible without the aid of religion, Wolff incurred the anger of his successor, Joachim Lange. As soon as Lange was installed as rector he asked members of the theological faculty to censure Wolff. This entire affair became serious when close military advisors to Frederick William I presented Wolff as a disciple of determinism, a theory which defended army deserters who were "determined" to desert. The king was furious and ordered Wolff out of the country on November 8, 1723. By 1729 even Wolff's textbooks were forbidden in Prussia. Wolff was seen by students throughout Germany as a man who was in step with the democratic spirit of the times. When the more open-minded Frederick the Great ascended to the throne in 1740 he asked Wolff to return to Prussia. Wolff was more than just a hero to the academic youth of Germany, and Kant later summed up Wolff's accomplishment best, calling him "the founder of the, up to now, unextinguished spirit of thoroughness in Germany."[27]

Wolff's influence was felt outside the philosophical realm. Bodmer and Breitinger dedicated Die Discourse der Mahlern to him, and other moral weeklies, such as La Belle Wolffienne, were full of ideas taken from Wolff (and Locke).[28] Gottsched was influenced by Wolff, comparing him to a ship's helmsman who brings a vessel through a stormy sea of conflicting ideas.[29] Ernst Gottlieb Baron was also a disciple. In his Untersuchung des Instruments der Lauten he asks who does not know of Wolff's teachings?[30] Before Wolff's influence on musical writers is discussed, some of Wolff's basic concepts, important for understanding German musical thought in the 1720s, should be mentioned.

Richard J. Blackwell, in his introduction to Wolff's Preliminary Discourse on Philosophy in General, calls him "a typical representative of the Enlightenment" who "sought a complete synthesis of all human knowledge."[31] The goal of Wolff's philosophy is to know things as they are, not just if things are possible, but why they are so. This attitude manifests itself in a pseudo-mathematical system of givens and results of propositions. His system resembles Hutcheson's "formulas" for various moral virtues presented in the _Essay Concerning Beauty_. As Lewis White Beck has said, Wolff maintained that "philosophy can imitate the connectedness of mathematics."[32] Wolff's approach to artistic matters was down-to-earth. The powers of the imagination (_Einbildungskraft_) were recognized as necessary for the creative process, but must not be confused with empty musings which are only a waste of time. The imagination, for Wolff, was valuable only as the first step in the creation of an artifact. It was not the mysterious, divine faculty for Wolff that it was for Francis Hutcheson, or Roger North.[33]

The major point which must be remembered, however, is not Wolff's specific attitude toward aesthetic questions but his view of the world. This was a curious mixture of rationalistic and empirical concepts which resulted in a highly intellectualized (and confused) system. Wolff's pedantic visions were popular in their day--perhaps the German-speaking world was ready for systems based on scientific, perhaps pseudo-scientific, precepts. His writings were also popular since they were written in German and seemed to support the movement away from unwanted foreign influences. In the end, we must give Wolff his due: "he was indeed _praeceptor Germaniae_, and most good things in German philosophy in the early eighteenth century came from this prosy, pretentious, slightly comical, professor."[34]

1 See William Bathe, <u>A Brief Introduction to the Skill of Song</u> (London, n.d.); Thomas Salmon, <u>Essay To The Advancement of Musick</u> (London, 1672); Lord Brouncker, <u>Renatus Descartes Excellent Compendium of Musick</u> (London, 1653). On British music in general during this period see W. T. Atcherson, "Seventeenth-Century Music Theory: England," <u>Journal of Music Theory</u>, 16 (1972), 6-15; Christopher Lewis, "Incipient Tonal Thought in Seventeenth-Century English Theory," <u>Studies in Music from Western Ontario</u>, 6 (1981), 24-46; Gertrude Miller, "Tonal Materials in Seventeenth-Century English Theorists" (Ph.D. dissertation, University of Rochester, 1960); Lavan Maesch, "A Survey of Musical Development in England from 1627 to 1660" (Master's thesis, University of Rochester, 1936.)

2 See Percy Scholes, <u>The Oxford Companion to Music</u> (London: Oxford University Press, 1950), 769. George Fox, founder of the Society of Friends, wrote in his Journal of 1649: "I was moved to cry out against all kinds of music."

3 Ibid., 766.

4 Max Caspar, "Johannes Keplers wissenschaftliche und philosophische Stellung," in <u>Kopernikus und Kepler</u> (Munich, 1943), 60.

5 See George Schoolfied, <u>The Figure of the Musician in German Literature</u> (Chapel Hill: University of North Carolina Press, 1956), xi; and the modern edition of Grimmelshausen's <u>Simplicissimus</u> by Rolf Tarot (Tübingen: Niemeyer, 1967).

6 See Richard Alewyn, <u>Johann Beer: Studien zum Roman des 17. Jahrhundert</u> (Leipzig, 1932); and Alewyn's preface to <u>Johann Beer, Sein Leben von ihm selbst erzählt</u> (Göttingen: Vandenhoeck & Ruprecht, 1965).

7 On the development of British journalism see Joseph Frank, <u>The Beginnings of the English Newspaper: 1620-1660</u> (Cambridge, Mass.: Harvard University Press, 1961).

8 J. W. H. Atkins, <u>Literary Criticism: 17th and 18th Centuries</u> (London: Methuen & Co., 1951), 147.

9 Edward A. Bloom and Lilian D. Bloom, eds., <u>Addison and Steele: The Critical Heritage</u> (London: Routledge and Kegan Paul, 1980), 1-7.

10 Ibid., 81.

11 See Robert M. Otten, Joseph Addison (Boston: Twayne, 1982), 172-176.

12 Ibid., 84.

13 Ibid., 68.

14 George Aitken, The Life of Richard Steele (London: Isbister, 1889), App. 2, 2:428-429.

15 Ben Franklin, "Idea of the English School, " in The Papers of Ben Franklin (New Haven: Yale University Press, 1961), 102-108.

16 C. S. Lewis, "Addison," in Eighteenth-Century English Literature: Modern Essays in Criticism (New York, Oxford University Press, 1959), 144-157.

17 Margaret Laurie, "Addison," in New Grove's Dictionary, 1, 104.

18 Ibid., 104.

19 Siegmund A. E. Betz, "The Operatic Criticism of the Tatler and Spectator," Musical Quarterly, XXXI (1945), 318.

20 Gloria Flaherty, Opera in the Development of German Critical Thought (Princeton: Princeton University Press, 1982), 83.

21 Lewis White Beck, Early German Philosophy (Cambridge, Mass.: Harvard University Press, 1969), 245-247.

22 Ibid., 246.

23 Ibid., 246.

24 G. Zart, Einfluß der englischen Philosophen seit Bacon auf die deutsche Philosophie des 18. Jahrhunderts (Berlin: Ferdinand Dümmler, 1881), 23.

25 Joachim Birke, Christian Wolffs Metaphysik und die zeitgenössische Literatur- und Musiktheorie: Gottsched, Scheibe, Mizler (Berlin: de Gruyter, 1966), 1.

26 See Beck, _Early German Philosophy_, 258-259.

27 Immanuel Kant, _Kritik der reinen Vernunft_ (Riga, 1781), preface to the 2nd ed.; see Beck, _Early German Philosophy_, 261: "Urheber des bisher noch nicht erloschenen Geistes der Gründlichkeit in Deutschland."

28 Beck, _Early German Philosophy_, 260.

29 Johann Christoph Gottsched, _Erste Gründe der gesammten Weltweisheit_ (2nd. ed.; Leipzig, 1736), 2.

30 Ernst Gottlieb Baron, _Untersuchung des Instruments der Lauten_ (Nuremberg, 1727), 2. See trans. by Douglas Alton Smith (Redondo Beach, California: Instrumenta Antiqua, 1976), 2. All translations of Baron will be taken from Smith's work.

31 Christian Wolff, _Preliminary Discourse on Philosophy in General_, trans. by Richard J. Blackwell (Indianapolis and New York: Bobbs-Merrill, 1963), viii.

32 Beck, _Early German Philosophy_, 262.

33 Christian Wolff, _Vernünfftige Gedancken von Gott_ (9th ed.; Halle, 1743), 807.

34 Beck, _Early German Philosophy_, 275.

CHAPTER III

CROSS-CURRENTS IN EARLY EIGHTEENTH-CENTURY MUSICAL THOUGHT

Any capable historian of the early eighteenth century is aware of the exchange of ideas which took place between men of ideas from different nations. It can come as no surprise that John Locke was well known in Germany, or that Shaftesbury's writings enjoyed a greater popularity on the continent than in his homeland. Even so, the degree of influence that British writers had on Germans was extraordinary, and while exchange in the other direction--from Germany to Britain--was less common, it did occur. (A previously unrecognized seventeenth-century example--Kircher's influence on John Milton--is discussed in Appendix I of this study.) Such cross-influences are made even more remarkable by the fact that these British and German writers had such diverse careers. Essayists, philosophers, music theorists, and performers all contributed to the foundation of early eighteenth-century musical thought. Joseph Addison influenced the writings of Mattheson and Scheibe to a surprising degree. Even a writer as little-known today as James Ralph was cited by J. C. Gottsched and Lorenz Mizler. The writings of Johann Mattheson had a direct impact on a Scottish writer on music, Alexander Malcolm. Within the boundaries of these nations such exchanges of ideas also occurred. Francis Hutcheson may have known Malcolm, and Mattheson was in close contact with every major writer on music in Germany. On a higher level there were other, less obvious influences, such as the admiration for the works of Christian Wolff shared by Gottsched, J. A. Scheibe, Ernst Gottlieb Baron, and Mizler. To know the work of one eighteenth century writer on musical thought is to know very little: there was a dense, and sometimes tangled, web of interrelationships and influences which has only begun to be unraveled.

Writers on Music in Britain

Joseph Addison

Few men reflected the temper of their times as did Joseph Addison (1672-1719). Born the son of an Anglican minister, Addison received all the benefits of his station, including a fine classical education at Oxford. After earning his M. A. degree in 1693, and holding some minor political offices, Addison took an extensive tour of the continent (discussed below). After returning from these travels he rose quickly in Whig political ranks, becoming Irish secretary to Lord Wharton. After the Tory victories in 1710 Addison lost his position and turned more and more to writing. Along with Richard Steele he edited a series of periodicals which made him famous. With the death of Queen Anne in 1714 Addison was again able to hold political office, and eventually became secretary of state under the Hanoverian, George I. Addison's abilities as an administrator, playwright, poet, and essayist, did not go unnoticed, as his final monument in Westminster Abbey shows. An even greater monument to him, however, was the admiration shown for his writings throughout Europe, especially in Germany.

Addison and Germany

Although his periodicals exerted considerable influence there, Addison's travels in Germany may also have had an impact on German musical writers. Between 1699 and 1703 Joseph Addison lived on the continent, his studies financed by the British government. It was the usual training given a young man interested in the foreign service.[1] Addison spent some time in France and met Boileau in 1700, a powerful influence on the Briton.[2] In their discussions Boileau not only emphasized the superiority of ancient writers, but also pointed out the difficulty of translating them. Though his meeting with Boileau was the highlight of his stay there, Addison's memories of the French nation reveal a considerable negative prejudice:

> The French are certainly the most implacable, and most dangerous enemies of the British nation. Their form of government, their religion, their jealousy of the British power, as well as their prosecutions of commerce, and pursuits of universal Monarchy, will fix them for ever in their animosities and aversion towards us, and make them catch at all opportunities of subverting our constitution, destroying our religion,

> ruining our trade, and sinking the figure which we make among the nations of Europe. 3

The good company and inspiring discussions with Boileau were not able to dispel the strong Francophobic bias that Addison had acquired in his homeland.

Addison's travels through Italy, Switzerland, and Austria finally led him to Dresden in the winter of 1703, where he was admitted to the Electoral court, meeting the Electress of Brandenburg and the Electorial Prince (later King William I of Prussia).[4] Addison met the British resident in Dresden, Lord Winchilsea, to whom Addison wrote several weeks later from Hamburg.[5] From the tone of the letter (it deals almost exclusively with wine-drinking) it can be assumed that Addison enjoyed those social activities which Hamburg had to offer.[6] Addison came to know John Wich, British resident in Hamburg with whose family Johann Mattheson was later associated. Wich had been born into the field of diplomacy. His father, Peter Wich, had been resident in Hamburg before him, and John became resident there in 1702.[7] There was a stronger connection between Wich and Addison, however, than just their nationality. Both men shared Sir Joseph Williamson, also a diplomat, as their godfather. Addison was most likely named after Sir Joseph, who was a good friend of Addison's father, Lancelot Addison.[8]

While in Hamburg it seems probable that Addison met Johann Mattheson, who was at that time a singer at the opera and close associate of Reinhard Keiser. Keiser was a frequent companion of Wich, who patronized the Hamburg opera heavily.[9] It seems likely that Addison would have heard at least one opera performance, although there is unfortunately no evidence of such an experience. During that year alone Keiser had three operas performed, Der verführte Claudius, Salomon, and Die Geburt der Minerva.[10] Wich's involvement in the Hamburg opera was not unusual as opera was heavily subsidized by foreign diplomats and businessmen who lived there. Between 1727 and 1729, for example, Cyrill Wich, John Wich's son and successor, was the director of the opera's financial affairs.[11]

What effect did his stay in Hamburg have on Addison? If he did see an opera there, or even if he discussed opera with John Wich, it must have left some trace. Addison's constant plea that opera in London be made somehow more "British" could well have been inspired by the thriving native opera tradition he saw in Hamburg. In any event, Addison made an impression on the Germans he met. The Electress wrote, in a letter to Leibniz from Dresden dated February 24, 1703, "Il est fort bon, et ce qui est plus extraordinaire, fort modeste poète..."[12] The impression the sophisticated Addison might have made upon the twenty-two year old Mattheson can only be imagined. Is there any reason to suspect that Mattheson knew Addison's work? We know that there is: Mattheson translated many of the Tatler and Spectator papers the same year that he published Das neu-eröffnete Orchestre. But there is in addition a considerable amount of circumstantial evidence to link the two, and several passages in Mattheson's work do indeed seem to owe something to Addison, as we shall see in our discussion of Mattheson.

Francis Hutcheson

The importance of Francis Hutcheson in the development of Enlightenment thought is now widely accepted by scholars.[13] Ernest Tuveson makes three important points about the philosopher. First, his greatest importance is to be found "in systematization rather than original contributions.[14] His Inquiry Into the Original of our Ideas of Beauty and Virtue of 1725 is an open defense of the principles of Shaftesbury, for example.[15] Second, his philosophical starting point, his attempt "to reconcile the two sources of the new morality--Shaftesbury and Addison," shows that he was in the mainstream of Enlightenment thought.[16] Third, "like all members of the Scottish philosophy-of-man school, Hutcheson owed his psychology ultimately to Locke."[17] Even so, Hutcheson was never a blind follower of these men, and he did make his own unique contributions.[18] His writings in the 1720s must be seen as the first effort at a system of aesthetics, and his attempt to make a "thorough empirical study of human nature" was combined with a love for beauty and a desire to explore man's appreciation of it.[19]

An important facet of Hutcheson's philosophy was his desire to provide an empirical analysis of human nature, "a study which was intended to illuminate God's purpose for man, not to replace it."[20] Critical of the dour Protestantism of his associates, Hutcheson's deep interest in beauty must be seen in the light of the religious and social climate of the time. Though we can reject W. R. Scott's assumption that beauty had been "banished" and the "whole sensuous man" martyrized, such currents did exist in Britain.[21] Hutcheson comments on the cause-effect attitudes of many of his contemporaries:

> We shall generally find in our modern philosophic Writtings, nothing further on this Head i.e., the "various Pleasures which human Nature is capable of receiving", than some bare Division of them into Sensible, and Rational, and some trite commonplace Arguments to prove the latter to be more valuable than the former. Our sensible Pleasures are slightly pass'd over, and explain'd only by some Instances in Tastes, Smells, Sounds, or such like, which Men of any tolerable Reflection generally look upon as very trifling Satisfactions. 22

Hutcheson's defense of the arts manifests itself in his frequent references to them. As Peter Kivy has pointed out, music appealed to Hutcheson since the philosopher felt that there were sensations produced by certain intervals (the third, fifth, octave, etc.) which could be measured mathematically.[23] Even so, Hutcheson's remarks about music reveal little understanding of the art. This is evident in his discussion of the beautiful "uniformity of music." Below is the 1725 version of this discussion from the Inquiry, with additions Hutcheson made a year later in brackets and replacing the phrases put here in parenthesis:

> Under Original Beauty we may include Harmony, or Beauty of Sound, if that Expression can be allow'd, because Harmony is not usually conceiv'd as an Imitation of any thing else. Harmony often raises Pleasure in those who know not what is the Occasion of it: And yet the Foundation of this Pleasure is known to be a sort of Uniformity. When the several Vibrations of one Note regularly coincide with the Vibration of another, they make an agreeable Composition; Thus the Vibrations of any one Note coincide in Time with (every second Vibration) two Vibrations of its Octave; and two Vibrations of any Note coincide with three of its Fifth; and so on in the rest of the Chords. (Now good Compositions, beside the Frequency of these Chords, must retain a general Unity of Key, an Uniformity among the Parts in Bars, Risings, Fallings, Closes.) Now no Composition can be harmonious, in which Notes are not, for the most part, dispos'd according to these

natural Proportions: besides which a due regard must be had to the Key with governs the Whole, and to the Time, and Humour, in which the Composition is begun; an inartificial change of any of which, will produce the greatest and most Discord.] The Necessity of this will appear, by observing the Dissonance which would arise from tacking Parts of different Tunes together as one, altho both were separately agreeable. A greater Uniformity is also observeable among the Basses, Tenors, Trebles of the same Tune. [There is, indeed, in the best Compositions, a mysterious Effect of Dischords; they often give as great Pleasure as continu'd Harmony: whether by refreshing the Ear with Variety, or by awaking the Attention, and enlivening the Relish for the succeeding Harmony of Concords; as Shades enliven and beautify Pictures; or by some other means, not yet known: Certain it is, however, that they have their Place, and some good Effect in our best Compositions.] 24

It seems obvious that after the 1725 edition of the Inquiry someone (perhaps Hutcheson himself) realized that these first remarks about music were poor work. The revised version seems to have been done under the watchful eye of a knowledgable musician, though no writer has commented on who this person might have been. (Kivy, indeed, is the only scholar to note the improvements, but he describes them as mere corrections of terminology.)[25] The logical choice for the influence on Hutcheson is Alexander Malcolm. Hutcheson may well have known him, for their biographies intersect in suggestive ways.[26] But even if they never met, Hutcheson must have known Malcolm's treatise on music, which had already appeared in 1721. How else can one explain the startling similarity between the "Dischords" insertion quoted above and the analogous passage in Malcolm:

The Harmony of Dischords is, that wherein the Dischords are made use of as a solid and substantial Part of

> Harmony; for by a proper Interposition of a Discord the succeeding Concords receive an additional Lustre. Thus the Dischords are in Musick what the strong Shades are in Painting; for as the Lights there, so the Concords here, appear infinitely more beautiful by the Opposition. 27

Whether or not Hutcheson relied on Malcolm for musical advice, Hutcheson's work is full of references to music. For Hutcheson, music was the perfect paradigm, an example to be included in his justification for certain philosophical attitudes. He even includes music in his discussions of his favorite theme, unity in variety. Many philosophers, Hutcheson says, only consider the most simple ideas of sensation when they discuss the pleasures of the senses. There are, however, more complex aspects to our appreciation of the beautiful. Just as a fine landscape painting is more attractive if it contains a variety of objects, not just with a clear sky, or an open plain, "so in Musick, the Pleasure of fine Composition is incomparably greater than that of any one Note, how sweet, full, or swelling soever."[28]

There is one other reason why Hutcheson's writings are of special interest to this study. Hutcheson's strong conviction (based on his reading of Shaftesbury) that there was indeed an analogy between beauty and moral virtue, as well as his uncompromising opposition to Hobbes' doctrine of self-interest (i.e., that our own self-love dictates all our actions) proved to have a great impact on German religious writers. Hutcheson's thought "so thoroughly represented the spirit of the age that, when it passed over into Germany, it penetrated not only into the sermons, but even into the catechisms and children's books (Kinderfreunde) of the rationalizing divines of that period."[29]

Alexander Malcolm

Alexander Malcolm's (1685-1763) slight reputation today rests on his Treatise of Musick: Speculative, Practical and Historical, a work which reveals the main interest of the writer was not music, but mathematics as well as theology. His chief mathematical contributions were his New Treatise on Arithmetic (1718) and New System of Arithmetic (1730). Malcolm was most frequently employed, however, as a protestant minister. He came to America in 1734 and was successful as a preacher, schoolmaster, and teacher of music.[30] He was rector at St. Michael's Church at Marblehead, Massachusetts from 1740 to 1749. Malcolm's final position was as rector at St. Paul's in Queen Anne's County, Maryland, a post he held from May 16, 1754 until his death.[31]

Unfortunately, there is little information on Malcolm's early life or education. He is referred to by his American contemporaries as a Master of Arts, but where Malcolm studied is not clear. His father was a minister, and Malcolm's upbringing must have included some study of music. It is possible that he studied with either of the two leading harpsichord teachers in Edinburgh early in the century, Crumbden or Beck--both of whom were of German origin.[32] In any event, Malcolm's training could hardly have been exhaustive. His treatise reveals an inquisitive and facile intellect but lacks the insight of the practicing musician. Most of his treatise is concerned with tuning, though he does take time to support the C-clef concepts of Thomas Salmon.[33] The treatise is the first work on music by a Scottish writer in the eighteenth century, and it is a valuable source for information on attitudes toward music during this period.

Malcolm's Treatise reveals that his most important sources of information were Descartes, Mersenne, and, interestingly enough, the Musurgia universalis of Athanasius Kircher. It is in his explanation of ancient harmonic practices that Malcolm includes his translations of ancient authors whose works were at that time available only in Meibom's Antiquae musicae auctores septem (Amsterdam, 1652). In passages dealing with historical matters Kircher is often cited, as in Malcolm's discussion of the origin of music, or his comments on ancient monuments.[34] Similarly, in a discussion on ancient instruments he concludes with the advice "if you are curious to hear more of this, and see the Figures of Instruments both ancient and modern, go to Mersennus and Kircher."[35] As frequently as Malcolm does refer to Kircher, however, the German is often taken to task for his illogical mathematical formulations concerning chord vibrations, consonance and dissonance, and temperaments.[36] Malcolm also ridicules Kircher's discussions of music as a remedy for serpent and spider bites.[37]

Despite his negative comments, the Musurgia must have been one of the inspirations for Malcolm's own efforts. The sight of such an attempt at a comprehensive approach to musical science must have convinced Malcolm of the feasibility of his own project. The use of Kircher's Musurgia made by Malcolm also serves to emphasize the fact that Malcolm was a well-read writer on music, if not a professional musician, and that the author was attempting to bring the new insights of his age into the realm of musical thought, as his references to Shaftesbury and Locke show. In the end, it is in his discussions on the affections and the imagination--and not his translations, as Karl Darenberg maintains--that Malcolm made his greatest contributions.[38]

Roger North

> His writings carry the forthright spirit of the 17th century into the more polite atmosphere of the 18th. Burney called him a "speculative dilettant", but he may also be called the first English music critic. 39

While one must agree that North's writings betray a seventeenth-century bias, John Wilson's decision to name him "the first English music critic" seems ill-advised. There are other writers who deserve the honor, writers whose works were published and who participated actively in the artistic scene. Roger North spent most of his life on his estates, having fallen from royal favor when James II fled the country in 1688.[40] North's essays are his personal observations on the areas of music he found interesting. His writings are rich in comments about the more general aspects of the musical art and not the prosaic matters which fascinated Malcolm. One can concur with Jamie Croy Kassler, who calls North's writings "a beautiful microcosm of the intellectual climate of opinion of his day: they illuminate questions posed in the 17th and early 18th centuries that writers endeavored to answer long after North's death."[41]

North and German Musicians

Roger North was influenced by several German musicians: Captain de Prendcourt, Gottfried Finger, Johann Ernst Galliard, and Johann Christoph Pepusch and, most extensively, Bernhardt Schmidt (c.1630-1708), known in Britain as Father Smith. Smith was an organ builder of some ability, trained in Germany and Holland, who came to Britain in 1666 and by 1681 was appointed King's Organ Maker.[42] He is probably best known for his role in the great "Battle of the Organs"--a contest between Smith and Renatus Harris to see which of them could produce the better instrument in the Temple church in London. North was one of the judges in this contest and was possibly Smith's strongest supporter.[43] After winning the contest Smith was acknowledged the best organ builder in the land.[44]

But Smith was more than just an organ builder. By the late 1690s he was a member of an exclusive club founded by Richard Bentley, a famous classical scholar and Royal Librarian. William Sumner tells us this club "consisted of a small group of intimate friends who met once or twice a week in his apartments at St. James's."[45] The original members were Bentley, John Evelyn, John Locke, Isaac Newton, Christopher Wren, all "names sufficient in themselves to render illustrious the age in which they lived, and the country which gave them birth."[46] Smith's membership was due to his expertise on acoustical matters, a subject of interest to Newton, who had been on the committee which planned for the organ at St. Paul's built by Smith. North's respect for Smith is demonstrated by the fact that when North decided to purchase Rougham Hall in Norfolk during 1690, he had Smith design and install an organ in the music room there.[47] North referred to this organ as "divine" and "an inexhaustible magazine" for "gratifying my continual thirst after Harmony."[48]

The second most important German in North's musical life was the mysterious Captain de Prendcourt (fl. 1686-1705). A harpsichordist (whose name was undoubtedly an alias), de Prendcourt had come to Britain during the reign of James II and served at court.[49] North transcribed Prendcourt's treatise on thoroughbass around 1710. The main focus of this work was on ornamentation. North was a friend and admirer of Prendcourt, though the latter had some unfortunate personal traits, including arrogance and dishonesty.[50] Even so, North was enthusiastic about his abilities as a performer and Prendcourt probably supplied North with his most vivid impressions of actual musical practice and music in general.[51]

Gottfried Finger (c.1660-1730) came to Britain in much the same manner as Prendcourt, as a musician in the chapel of James II.[52] North's references to him concern Finger's participation in a London contest held in 1700 which was meant to decide who was the best composer in Britain. Finger placed fourth (behind John Weldon, John Eccles, and Daniel Purcell)--a judgement which North found unfair.[53] "Mr. G. Finger," notes North "a German and a good musitian...went away upon it; declaring that he thought he was to compose musick for men, and not for boys."[54] North esteemed Finger as an able composer, unjustly treated (considering North's own political fate, he may have identified with Finger as well).

A more direct role was played by J. E. Galliard (1687-1749), who came to Britain around 1706 and is mentioned by North in his 1710 essay "What is Ayre?"[55] "The great Master Galliard" is invoked during a discussion on syncopation and harmonic movement. Since North was also one of the subscribers to Galliard's cantata <u>The Hymn of</u>

Adam and Eve (1728), it seems likely the men knew one another. Roger North's relationship with J. C. Pepusch (1667-1752) is easier to document. Pepusch had come to Britain from Saxony around 1704 and was an important force in British musical life during the early eighteenth century. In writing his "The Theory of Sounds" North became interested in a question concerning arithmetical ratios and musical intervals. To resolve the question he wrote to Pepusch. Sir John Hawkins, who studied the papers of Pepusch in the course of writing his History of Music, pointed out that he found a letter from North as well as an answer by the German.[56] British aristocrat-dilettante that he was, North still did not live isolated from the currents of the musical world. More importantly, if North's experiences can be seen as typical, German influence on British musical thought seems to have been considerable.

James Ralph

James Ralph travelled to London from America in 1724, having left his wife and position in Philadelphia, to seek his fortune in Britain.[57] Benjamin Franklin, who met the young writer in Philadelphia, allowed Ralph to accompany him on the trip. Once in Britain Ralph was supported for a time by Franklin, but their friendship came to an abrupt end when Franklin made improper advances to Ralph's mistress, which she rejected. Franklin was relieved to be done with Ralph, however, for the latter had run up debts and the friendship had soured. Still, Franklin was able to evaluate Ralph positively, calling him "ingenious, genteel in his manners and extremely eloquent.[58]

This eloquence is apparent in the Touchstone: or, Historical, Critical, Political, and Theological Essays on the reigning Diversions of the Town (London, 1728). A guide to cultural life in London, the book possesses a charm and wit which must have exerted a powerful influence on its readers. It is not difficult to understand why Fielding and the librettist-poet Henry Carey fell under Ralph's spell.[59] The Touchstone is important for these reasons, but also because the author makes many observations about opera in London in the 1720s. As a mirror of its times, the Touchstone stands unsurpassed. Ralph represents the early Enlightenment at its cocky best, with just the proper amount of sincerity. His thought is often subtle and perceptive, and one regrets that his writings were not widely distributed. He remained in the public eye after the 1720s, primarily as a political satirist. His bitter poem attacking Pope's Dunciad (1728) also insulted Swift and Gay and did much to ruin his hopes for literary fame.[60]

Johann Christoph Pepusch

By almost any measure, Pepusch was a powerful force in the musical life of Britain. Granted a Doctor of Music degree from Oxford (1713), collaborator with John Gay on The Beggar's Opera, and member of the Royal Society (1745), Pepusch was well-known as a musician and intellectual.[61] Though this broad range of interests made him a popular figure, Pepusch's position was greatly aided by his marriage to the wealthy soprano Marguerite de l'Epine around 1720, a marriage which enabled him to indulge in his antiquarian proclivities.[62] Pepusch was one of the first true musician-scholars in eighteenth-century Britain and was partially responsible for developing wider interest in the performance of older music.

Although respected as a theorist, the only work of any substance he published was A Treatise of Harmony (1731). This work, a curious mixture of modern and obsolete concepts is, as Louis Chenette has noted, "disappointingly brief, in view of the high esteem with which he was held as a teacher and theorist."[63] Pepusch was considered something of a pedant by his contemporaries, however, and Burney later accused him of having "fettered the genius of his scholars by antiquainted rules."[64] Pepusch's affection for antiquity manifested itself in a love for "Greek genera, scales, diagrams, geometrical, arithmetical, and harmonical proportions; quantities, apotomes, lemmas, and everything concerning ancient harmonies that was dark, unintelligible, and foreign to common and useful practice."[65]

Of course, one must remember that Pepusch, born in 1667, was no child of the Enlightenment. This is reflected by his love for Corelli, his conservative opinions on the use of hexachords, and his essentially modal conception of counterpoint.[66] It should also be remembered that he was rewarded, not condemned, for his interest in ancient music: his admittance to the Royal Society came after a speech on Greek musical theory.[67] Though he was a powerful influence on musical thought in the 1730s, he was not forward-looking, and represents a good example of why discussions of "trends" in musical thought can be misleading. Certainly, he had important things to say on many matters--and a wide audience. Yet, he is rarely considered in discussions of musical thought in the eighteenth century.

Pepusch is at his most antique in his attack upon Alexander Malcolm, whom he accuses of downplaying the importance of the hexachord system because the Scotsman was unacquainted with using them.[68] Pepusch's attempts to reconcile modern musical practice with the hexachord system are the most obvious manifestations of his conservative bias. Schooled in the system of the German Baroque, and twenty years older than Mattheson, one could hardly expect Pepusch to be in step with his times. As a writer on music, at least, he was unoriginal and out of date. Even so, his importance in British musical life during the 1730s was great.

Johann Friedrich Lampe

Unlike Pepusch, John Frederick (Johann Friedrich) Lampe expressed himself in English with ease and seems to have enjoyed writing about the musical art in less specific, but often more meaningful terms. His two small treatises, A Plain and Comprehensive Method of Teaching Thorough Bass and The Art of Musick comprise a complete harmonic system, as Chenette has observed.[69] More than this, Lampe's writings contain some of the most interesting observations on music made in the English language in the 1730s. His clear prose style and his thoughtful outlooks place him in the mainstream of early Enlightenment thought. Significantly, the best writer on music in Britain during the 1730s was a German.

Lampe was born in Saxony and educated at the university of Helmstedt. He came to Britain in 1725 as a bassoonist in the King's Theater.[70] Lampe played in various theater orchestras during the next years. He eventually became a composer for pantomimes and musicals, scoring his greatest success with Henry Carey in The Dragon of Wantley in 1737.[71] A year later Lampe married Isabella Young, sister of Thomas Arne's wife and both daughters of Charles Young. In later life Lampe became a close friend of Charles Wesley, who wrote a hymn on Lampe's death in 1751. Lampe was an individual of fine personal character and a philosophical nature, traits admirably reflected in his writings.[72]

Lampe makes it clear in both his major works that he has something new to say. In the Method he dismisses all previous texts on the subject of thoroughbass. "As to the Pieces already in Print," Lampe notes, "I need not say much, since Masters can make but little, and Scholars [i.e., students] no Use of them."[73] Lampe's antipathy for earlier writers, particularly Pepusch, is obvious in The Art of Musick.

To Lampe, Pepusch represented all that was unnatural in music. Pepusch, who gloried in mathematical calculations and proposed a revitalization of the hexachord system, was, in Lampe's view, a victim of the same mistakes made by the ancients. The "manifest Blunders" which Lampe claimed to find in Pepusch's treatise were the same, or similar, to those made by the ancients, who "took their first Principles from the Mathematicks, and by endeavouring to make Musick subservient to Numbers and Lines, and by calculating Proportions, have done themselves infinite Prejudice."[74] Lampe felt that music had to be based on other principles, and attempted to discover them in nature, that is, in the natural harmonics of the vibrating string.[75] As Chenette has observed, by using the overtone system to proclaim the rule of nature, Lampe merely substituted one rationalistic hierarchy for another.[76] Still, Lampe's rejection of Pepusch was significant and reminds one of Mattheson's rejection of earlier writers in Das forschende Orchestre, where fidelity to nature is the often mentioned goal of all the arts. This similarity is more striking when one sees that Lampe insists over and over again that the final judge of musical matters must be the ear, and cites Locke to support his theories on the importance of sense experience.[77] For these reasons, and because Lampe cites Mattheson's Orchestre in The Art of Musick, it seems safe to assume that Mattheson's work exerted an influence on Lampe.[78] Louis Chenette makes a strong case for Rameau's influence on Lampe but does not even mention Mattheson's impact, which in the final analysis would seem to have been just as powerful, if not more so.[79]

Writers on Music in Germany

Johann Mattheson: Critic on Music and Society

It is difficult to summarize the life of Mattheson and his impact on the development of musical thought in Germany.[80] This is partially due to the fact that Mattheson never confined his activities soley to music. A composer and performing musician in his own right, Mattheson also took an active interest in politics, religion and the cultural life of his native Hamburg. In his writings Mattheson followed the tradition of Printz and Werckmeister, attempting to be philosophical and entertaining. He was a commentator of his times, a highly versatile and energetic critic of early eighteenth-century society. This versatility can be seen in his first major work, Das neu-eröffnete Orchestre (Hamburg, 1713), one of the most important books on music published in the early eighteenth century.[81] This work was not intended to be a treatise merely for the professional musician. Mattheson also wrote for the Galant Homme and the lady of fashion.[82] His frequent references to the Galant Homme and goût are not meant for effect alone, but reveal Mattheson's "enlightened" attitude toward music. It was no longer enough that art praise the Creator, it must do so in a tasteful manner. Similarly, Orchestre is used because Mattheson wished the word to indicate all types of music, i.e., theatrical, sacred, vocal, and instrumental, as well as musicial instruments.[83]

The main body of Mattheson's treatise is divided into three large sections: first, "on those things and symbols proper to musical composition"; second, "on musical composition and counterpoint itself"; and third, "how one judges one and another thing in music."[84] The tone of Mattheson's work is instructional. The chapters define general principles of music, terms and symbols in dictionary-like fashion, and his comments on aesthetic matters, which will provide the basis for our discussion of his thought in the first decades of the century, are scattered throughout the work.

Johann Mattheson and Britain

There is no other eighteenth-century writer on music more influenced by British thought and manners than Johann Mattheson. The biographical information shows that

Mattheson's British contacts were remarkably strong. Tutor to Cyrill Wich, the son of Sir John Wich, then personal secretary to the father, who became Envoy Extraordinary in 1709, Mattheson became secretary to Cyrill when he took his father's position in 1714.[85] During Mattheson's life-long association with the Wich family (he remained secretary until Cyrill was transferred to St. Petersburg in 1744) he "immersed himself in the study of the English language, English law, politics and economics; he became an expert in the intricate details of trade between England and Hamburg."[86] Another British factor in Mattheson's life which should not be underestimated was his wife, Catharina Jennings.[87] Finally, Mattheson was fluent in English and was a voracious reader of British authors--scientific, musical, or otherwise. He also translated dozens of English works into German.

It is in the capacity of translator that Mattheson offers the most convincing proof of his interest in British thought. Die Vernünftler was a selection of papers taken by Mattheson from the popular British periodicals and offered in translation. Borrowing his ideas from Addison and Steele, Mattheson adapted the Spectator and Tatler essays to his own purposes.[88] There could hardly be a better example of the type of influence that British culture had upon musical thought in Germany than the fact that Mattheson was the first German translator of the Spectator and Tatler.

There are even some similarities between the writings of Addison and Mattheson. The first involves a similarity of literary style. These stylistic similarities are difficult to discuss, however, since the two wrote in different languages. The importance of Addison in the development of the topical essay is well-known. Similarly important was the liaison which the Spectator created between literature and periodical writing.[89] Addison wrote in an entertaining style which captivated contemporary readers and set a new standard in periodical writings. Mattheson's place in German literary history is similar.[90] The dense, flat-footed style of many German and British writers around 1700 was soon to give way to a fluent prose style which was so much a part of the Enlightenment.

Another similarity between the two men, and one easier to describe, involves the use by both of systems of comparison, presentation of an idea by comparing the attitudes or practices in different countries to support an argument. Addison does this in Spectator No. 29 when presenting his attitude that recitative should fit the language of the audience. Mattheson's discussion of the merits of each country's musical traits is similar in construction. It is a device which one finds again and again in their works. Of course, Addison did not originate the technique, and Mattheson could have developed it from another source. In any event, Mattheson's discussion of the various temperaments of audience members, for example, or Addison's comments on languages and passions during his discussion on recitative, are constructed similarly. Other similarities between the works of the two men only underscore the essential point: Mattheson was heavily influenced by Joseph Addison in particular and British thought in general.

Johann Mattheson in the 1720s

During the 1720s, Mattheson discussed aesthetic issues most fully. Some ideas touched upon in Das neu-eröffnete

Orchestre are developed and given depth, others are rejected. Just as his work in each decade has its own specific character, each of Mattheson's major writings on music in the 1720s are unique. Das forschende Orchestre (1721) is the final installment in the Orchestre series (the first being Das neu-eröffnete Orchestre, and the second Das beschützte Orchestre of 1717). Das forschende Orchestre is similar to its predecessors, encyclopedic in scope although it purports to be a study first of the senses and music and secondly a defence of the interval of the fourth.[91]

The Critica Musica--24 issues printed between 1722 and 1725--was the first musical periodical in Germany.[92] A great financial success for Mattheson, each issue concluded with a gossipy account of musical happenings in European centers and was written in an entertaining prose style. Der musikalische Patriot (1728) represents a step away from the secular orientation of the Critica Musica and focuses primarily on the defense of the theatrical style in church music, and the Hamburg opera. While Cannon disagrees with Goldschmidt's view that the Patriot represents the beginning of "something of a retrogressive development" in Mattheson's attitudes, neither view may be totally correct.[93] Goldschmidt's contention is based on his own positivistic bias. Cannon's opinion that the Patriot shows a "development" in Mattheson's thought is not completely accurate. He did develop, but this development involved ideas about music and religion which were out of step with the secular trends of the 1720s. The Patriot represents what is old in Mattheson, and coincides with his decision of 1728 to leave active musical practice, a decision motivated by his increasing deafness. Because of this, the work will not be considered in our discussion of aesthetic issues.

Mattheson's major writings of the 1720s contain references to three personalities of some importance to this study: Locke, Malcolm, and Christian Wolff. While some of Mattheson's references to Locke in Das forschende Orchestre are discussed in later chapters, Appendix II of this study lists all of them. The two other fascinating influences on Mattheson--Wolff and Malcolm--must be discussed in more detail.

Mattheson and Christian Wolff

Mattheson's first reference to Wolff in Das forschende Orchestre is critical. Wolff's mathematical treatise contains no references to music, Mattheson notes, but a new edition should correct the oversight.[94] Wolff's lack of interest in music was a disappointment to Mattheson, which may explain his caustic response to Heinrich Bokemeyer, who cited Wolff in a long discussion on canon reproduced in Critica Musica. Bokemeyer held Wolff up as the authority who has proven that "syllogisms truly remain the only method of discovering the truth."[95] This comment could also be made about Mattheson's work, since he, like Wolff, never seems to have understood the difference between a proposition which is rational because it is produced by a correctly formulated syllogism and one which is rational because it is constructed from correct observation.[96] This can be supported by the fact that Mattheson, who corrects Bokemeyer on every point of error in his own footnotes to the latter's article, lets the comment on truth and syllogisms pass without comment.

Critical references to Wolff are found in <u>Der musikalische Patriot</u>, where Mattheson takes the hapless philosopher to task for his insensitive remarks about music in the <u>Vernünfftige Gedancken von dem gesellschaftlichen Leben der Menschen</u> (1721). The following remarks from <u>Patriot</u> are typical:

> What use is it, if it stands written in the Wolffian <u>Politics</u>, p. 385: "Music is for the pleasing of the ears, both instrumental and vocal." almost anyone could judge so artfully, having studied no science at all; not everyone knows that music belongs to building of the soul and virtue. So might a <u>Politicus</u> and <u>Philosophos</u> justly speak--[but] what is he doing talking of ears? Further, the famous Wolff states: "one would, to this end, require musicians in the community, who at occasions may create a pleasure for the ear." This is a very pedestrian, and not even the true point of music, in as much as it serves the community good; this system would be of support to every beer-fiddler.
>
> Mr. Wolff further states: "One knows from experience that nothing stays in the memory better than sung verse, and that music is well able to arouse all manner of Affections, which may connect the rules of virtue and proper behaviour with the affections, etc." Does music then just provide enjoyment for the ears? The author praises himself and states on various occasions "After my manner, after my manner thoroughly." Whoever wishes to have an example of this read his words on page 85, where it says: "It is often better that the parents learn their children to make money and to correctly use it. etc." But, not only is it always best and not just often; it should correctly [i.e., grammatically] be stated that parents teach children (not learn) how to make money, and with that how to use it correctly. This little side-dish is offered as an example of "clarity."
>
> What is further strongly stated about the misuse of music --and also intentionally interlarded with "lasciviousness and voluptuousness etc.," is the same old endless song. And my! Does the good, well-educated Wolff pay the slightest honor in his above-mentioned remarks on music, since he places on page 384 those

> most interested in music, those connected with opera, the true Academicos musicos (with necessary exceptions) rightly in a class with the dissipated pocket-players and has added a big et cetera. 97

It should be noted in Wolff's defense that he was actually positive about music. Unlike Locke (whose remarks about music were even less welcome to Mattheson), Wolff did acknowledge music as a force capable of influencing manners and politics.[98] Of course, Wolff's comments are brief and Mattheson was no doubt upset that the philosopher had so little to say about music. It should also be noted that Wolff's influence on Mattheson (and other German writers) was less in the realm of music than in approaches taken to specific problems. Both men saw themselves as "enlighteners" and attempted to bring the light of clarity to the darkness of ignorance they felt covered their respective fields.

Mattheson and Alexander Malcolm

> A Scottish author, Malcolm by name, has written a chapter on this [i.e., melody] and, indeed, at my suggestion; I have corresponded with him on this matter several years. 99

This quotation, and others in Critica Musica, make it clear that Mattheson was in communication with Malcolm during the early twenties. Mattheson, who later refers to Malcolm as a "learned Scottish nobleman", seems to have been fond of the Scotsman and his Treatise of Musick--a work which receives high praise in Critica Musica. Mattheson also provides information on music in Britain which shows familiarity not only with Malcolm's work but also Christopher Simpson's Compendium (London, 1667),

William Holder's Treatise (London, 1694), and Godfry Keller's Method (London, c. 1715).[100]

Although it would be rewarding to cite all the similarities between Mattheson's and Malcolm's works, such an attempt is beyond the scope of this study. One example, however, seems exceptionally interesting. It has already been mentioned that Malcolm may have exerted an influence on Hutcheson, particularly in the comparison of dissonance and consonance to darkness and light. Mattheson cites the following passage from Werckmeister in Das forschende Orchestre:

> How could one appreciate the day if no uncomfortable, yet bearably dark night came in between? ...When there are more dissonances than consonances, and these last longer and are not even resolved, then this is annoying and against nature. 101

Mattheson also cites Printz:

> Dissonances are [like] the darkness (I would rather say shadows), consonances like light. Light would not be so comfortable if it were always day, and never night. 102

It seems likely, on the basis of these statements, that Mattheson may have brought these analogies to the attention of Malcolm, who in turn may have influenced Hutcheson. Mattheson's Der vollkommene Capellmeister also contains specific reference to Malcolm, in this case the Scotsman's support of Mattheson's views on melodic writing.[103] The relationship between the two men (which probably ended when Malcolm left Britain, four years before the publication of Capellmeister) provides an important example of the exchange of musical thought between Britain and Germany.

Johann Mattheson in the 1730s

In the early part of the 1730s Mattheson was kept busy by his work for the *Niedersächsische Nachrichten von Gelehrte Sachen*.[104] Significantly, his assigned task was to report on the latest literary news from Britain. During this period he also translated important British works, including Elizabeth Rowe's *Friendship in Death* and *Bishop Burnet's History of His Own Time*.[105] In 1735 Mattheson published his *Kleine General-Baß Schule*, a work which contained an attack on the religious establishment of Hamburg for its lack of support for good church music.[106] With the publication in 1738 of *Der vollkommene Capellmeister*, Mattheson summarized his thought from earlier decades, but with a universality of scope and intent which was unprecedented. Despite the popularity of *Capellmeister* and his other works of the 1730s, acclaim for Mattheson was not universal. Two writers important to this study, Johann Adolph Scheibe and Lorenz Mizler, were critical of Mattheson, a situation which Mattheson aggravated by his insensitivity to the younger men's egos. Even so, considering the severity of many of the attacks on him, Mattheson showed remarkable self-control, especially since he was certainly afraid of losing his position as the leading writer on music in German.

Though Scheibe was positive towards Mattheson in a testimonial written for *Kern melodischer Wissenschaft* (Hamburg, 1738), problems arose when Mattheson accused him of stealing the title for his *Critischer Musicus* from Mattheson's *Critica musica*.[107] Scheibe responded that he had named his periodical after Gottsched's *Critischer Dichtkunst*, an admission which did not improve matters and led to a bitter feud.[108] By the next decade Scheibe went so far as to accuse Mattheson of being an impediment to musical progress.[109] It must be remembered, however, that despite their differences, Scheibe did owe Mattheson a debt, as many of his ideas were taken (consciously or unconsciously) from Mattheson.

Mattheson's relationship with Mizler was equally strained, but for different reasons. Not only was there a personal animosity between them, but they differed on important musical issues.[110] The important disagreement between the two involved their respective conceptions on what constituted the "natural" in music. This conflict manifested itself clearly in Mattheson's preface to Capellmeister, where he accused Mizler of having stolen his ideas on the relationship between sound and physiological changes.[111] Along with this criticism was a condemnation of those who approached music too mathematically--of course, Mizler was again the target. Mattheson later praised Mizler for using Das neu-eröffnete Orchestre as a textbook for his course in Leipzig.[112] For his part, Mizler included sections of Capellmeister in his Bibliothek, criticizing Mattheson on matters from celestial music to his inclusion of poems by John Milton in his treatise.[113] While we may never know the origin of all the disagreements that Mattheson had with Scheibe and Mizler, they do show us that musical thought in Germany during this period was not unified, and that, whether the three men wished to admit it or not, Mattheson was the person most responsible for the younger men's successes as writers on musical thought.

Johann David Heinichen

Of all the writers examined in this chapter, Johann David Heinichen (1683-1729) represents the most happy blend of practical musicianship and philosophical insight. Trained as a lawyer, Heinichen decided around 1708 for a career in music.[114] Esteemed as a composer in his lifetime, Heinichen's greatest contribution is his treatise Der General-Baß in der Composition, a greatly expanded version of his 1711 publication on thoroughbass.[115] Though his interests were not as wide-ranging as Mattheson's, Heinichen's work reveals a perceptive intellect. Interestingly enough, Mattheson's ideas had a considerable impact on Heinichen's attitudes about the importance of sense experience and the place of rhetoric in the art of musical composition.

The friendship between Mattheson and Heinichen began no later than 1717, when Mattheson appealed to Heinichen for an autobiographical sketch to be used in Das beschützte Orchestre.[116] Heinichen never provided the sketch, but he did respond when asked by Mattheson to comment on the ideas of Heinrich Bokemeyer in Critica Musica. In this response Heinichen revealed himself as a supporter of Mattheson. Thus Heinichen's basic point of departure, even before Der General-Baß, was essentially progressive and Matthesonian. This helps to explain why the two men got along as well as they did, which in the early eighteenth century meant reasonably well. German theorists and composers of this period argued with one another so often that no relationship, however good, was unclouded. Heinichen's references to Mattheson in Der General-Baß are not always complimentary. Heinichen ridicules Mattheson's circle of thirds (and proposes his circle of fifths), describing it as an "obscure scheme" which could not be supported by the final judge, the ear.[117] This criticism is a telling one since it was the glorification of the empirical (i.e., the ear) which preoccupied Mattheson in Das forschende Orchestre. No criticism could have devastated Mattheson more. For his part, Mattheson seems to have been willing to ignore this remark, and, even after Heinichen's death, referred to him with respect.[118]

Heinichen's indebtedness to Mattheson in Der General-Baß is obvious in passages which deal with more philosophical matters, especially in the introduction of the work. The following excerpt is typical:

> All arts and sciences have their rules, and must be learned through rules if we wish to avoid being pure naturalists, that is, half-ignorants. Yet we must avoid creating too many useless rules; even less must we so barbarously follow the questionable word "rule" so as if we would wish to be great rule-smiths, and to regulate even nature. No! all our useful rules must in the first place be taken from nature itself, her will, leanings, and character must be examined in all Gradibus, and observed cum submissione, so to speak: from their observations we should begin to take our rules. 119

One notices here the characteristic support of nature as the final authority on all matters of rule making and the similarity between the writing styles of Heinichen and Mattheson. Heinichen drops this style of writing when he leaves the realm of musical philosophizing and returns to more mundane matters, a fact which also indicates his debt to Mattheson. Heinichen's Lockian attitudes, perhaps taken from Mattheson, could also have been the product of his studies at the University of Leipzig (1702-1706).[120] It is possible that Heinichen studied under Christian Wolff, who was a <u>Privat-Dozent</u> there from 1703-1706.[121] Unfortunately, none of Heinichen's writings I have examined make reference to Wolff. It is unthinkable, however, that Heinichen was not aware of the famous philosopher.

Ernst Gottlieb Baron

> Why should it not do to bring more clarity to music than has been accomplished with philosophy? To whom are the writings of the illustrious Herr von Leibnitz, of the excellent Privy Councillor Thomasius, and the famous <u>Hofrat</u> Wolff not known? These writers translated all metaphysical technical terms and exorcisms of the academic spirits, dangerous as they may have sounded, into the best High German. If it is appropriate in these subjects, which was previously thought unbelievable, why should it not be similarly appropriate in music? 122

These words, taken from the preface of Baron's <u>Untersuchung des Instruments der Lauten</u> of 1727, typify the writer's major preoccupation: bringing clarity to the discussion of musical art. Baron cites the most important German philosophers of his day, Leibniz, Christian Thomasius, and Wolff. One assumes that the works which were helpful in "exorcisms of academic spirits" were Wolff's very popular treatises, for with Baron we are confronted with one of the most "Wolffian" of all writers on music. Not only did Baron cite Wolff in his <u>Untersuchung</u>, he incorporated the method of the philosopher in an unmistakeable manner. This can even be seen in his discussion of the terms selected for study, though Baron --like Heinichen--chose to avoid discussing imitation.

Baron (1696-1760), the son of an army officer, was educated at the University of Leipzig from 1715-1719.[123]

Here he studied law and philosophy and probably came under the influence of the writings of Wolff, whose works were used as texts at many universities. Baron then became a travelling lute virtuoso, feeling the call to music stronger than that to law. The high point of his career was his appointment in 1737 to the royal chamber and chapel orchestra of Crown Prince Frederick (later Frederick the Great). Baron remained in Berlin until his death, numbering among his acquaintances J. J. Quantz, Carl Heinrich Graun, and C. P. E. Bach.

Joachim Birke includes Baron's Abriß einer Abhandlung von der Melodie (Berlin, 1756) as an appendix in his work on Wolff and German writers on music.[124] Baron's essay is a clear example of how Wolff's method, which hinged upon a series of propositions and axioms, was taken up by a writer on music. The following is a brief example:

> For the creation of a good melody it requires:
> 1. a good natural disposition which
>   a. exists in a good understanding, namely, in the capacity to clearly imagine all things possible in music,
>   b. also in wit, which is the readiness to realize similarities, and whoever has this is sensitive and capable of remarkable invention,
>   c. also imagination, which is a strength of the soul to imagine melodies and their accompaniments with ease,
>   d. also critical ability, through which one differentiates, what belongs to a thing and what does not, what its properties are and are not, and how it differs form other things.
> 2. Cultivation, which must happen
>   *through the keyboard, because all harmony is found therein, at which one
>   1. must begin with small melodies and then
>   2. gradually build up to longer melodies and to get ideas from melodies, and then
>   3. the thoroughbass will be set as the basis, through which one learns

a) consonants and
b) dissonances, also their use and then
c) complete harmony.

*Practice. For if one begins to create small melodies, then one should try first with small galant pieces, until he reaches by and by a higher science, where he has to take into consideration
1. the recognition of key
2. their typical semitones
3. their modulations and
4. the art of subtly returning to a key. 125

This type of deductive scheme is not seen in Baron's Untersuchung, but the same interest in clarity is. Indeed, the highest complement Baron could pay to Heinichen's thoroughbass method was on the clarity with which the latter presented his ideas. It is Heinichen, he notes, who has "written the most plainly, clearly, and completely of all."[126]

Johann Adolph Scheibe

Scheibe seems to have transcended the fate he suffered at the hands of nineteenth-century musicologists. Once known only as the attacker of J. S. Bach, Scheibe is beginning to receive the attention he deserves. Two American dissertations in the early 1960s, and Benary's work on the Compendium musices, have done much to bring Scheibe into historical perspective.[127] Even so, George Buelow, in his recent entry in the New Grove's Dictionary, is forced to bemoan Scheibe's obscurity as a composer and writer on music.[128] Although no intellectual of the caliber of Wolff, Scheibe was a gifted writer on music who re-thought the ideas of music held by the previous generation and was not afraid to formulate new ones.

There were three important influences on Scheibe during the first thirty years of his life: his father, his studies at the University of Leipzig, and his relationship with Telemann. As a university student at Leipzig Scheibe came to know and admire Gottsched, then a professor of philosophy there. It was also in Leipzig that he began his relationship with Telemann, who became a close friend and encouraged Scheibe in his career as a writer on music. Scheibe's father, an organ builder of some repute, insisted that he prepare for a legal career and had his son educated at the *Nicolaikirche*. This education revolved around the study of classical Latin writers and training in rhetoric. Thus Scheibe received the same type of education as Mattheson and Heinichen, though the influence of Wolff and Gottsched were more important to him. Scheibe supported his attack on Bach, for example, with the intricate philosophical vocabulary and method developed by Wolff and disseminated by Gottsched. In the 1730s Scheibe attempted to incorporate the ideas of Gottsched and Wolff into his own aesthetic system, though in the process he refuted some of the most essential tenets of both men's outlooks. Though he failed in his attempt to provide a systematic approach to musical thought, he was one of the first to attempt it. Certainly there is no lack of material to examine, as Scheibe wrote profusely on all four of aesthetic issues discussed in this study.

Lorenz Christoph Mizler

Lorenz Mizler is difficult to place into historical perspective. We can only discuss some of the influences which caused him to write about music as he did. His periodical, Die neu-eröffnete musikalische Bibliothek, and his other works (notably his translation of Fux's Gradus ad Parnassum (Leipzig, 1742), reveal a many-sided intellect. The son of a court official at Heidenheim, Mizler received an excellent education in the Gymnasium at Ansbach, where he studied with Johann Matthias Gesner, who later became the director of the Leipzig Thomasschule.[129] In 1731 Mizler enrolled at the University of Leipzig where, as a pupil of Gottsched, he became enamored of the works of Wolff. During this period he also became a friend of J. S. Bach. In his master's thesis (dedicated to Mattheson), Quod musica ars sit pars eruditionis philosophicae (1734) Mizler presented ideas which were to dominate his thoughts for the rest of his life.[130] This included his desire to make the art of music a science by creating a theoretical basis which would make a systematic education in it possible for the first time.[131] By 1736 Mizler was lecturing on music at the university, using Mattheson's Neu-eröffnetes Orchestre as his text, and publishing a similarly titled periodical of his own, Die neu-eröffnete musikalische Bibliothek. By 1738 Mizler had founded the Korrespondierende Sozietät der musikalischen Wissenschaften which eventually included Telemann, G. H. Stölzel, Handel, and J. S. Bach. Though his medical career superseded his musical activities in later years, he did continue publishing his periodical and other works, including his translation of Fux.[132]

The Bibliothek (appearing from 1736-1754) contains a wide variety of material, including excerpts from works by Printz, Mattheson, Scheibe, and Fux as well as literary authorities such as Gottsched. Gottsched's comments, taken from Critische Dichtkunst, deal with opera, ode, and cantata and are all commented upon by Mizler in footnotes.

The Bibliothek also contains reports on current musical events throughout Germany at the end of certain numbers, much like Mattheson's Critica musica. Though the Bibliothek shows the influence of Leibniz, Wolff, Gottsched, and Mattheson, Mizler often criticized the ideas of contributors, particularly Gottsched and Mattheson. He disagreed with Gottsched's stand on opera and rejected Mattheson's skepticism about the importance of mathematics in music. Mizler was fascinated by this latter topic, adopting Leibniz's attitude that music involved an "unconscious counting" of the soul.[133] Taking his cue from Wolff, who had attempted to show that all things could be related to mathematical models, Mizler made the study of Wolff's works a requirement in his regulations for a "Society of Musical Sciences," and noted that he would "show the use of Wolff's philosophy in music in a special work: de usu ac praestantis philosophiae Wolfianae in musicae."[134] Though he never seems to have written the work, the intent is a clear proof that Mizler found the concepts of Wolff more adapatable to a philosophy of the arts than had Gottsched or Scheibe.[135]

Gottsched's influence on Mizler was a profound one. Although he had no patience with Gottsched's hostile attitudes toward opera, Mizler never attacked his writing style or literary tenets.[136] For Mizler, Gottsched was a model Wolffian in literature, just as he wished to be one in music. Mizler used Gottsched's love of thoroughness (Gründlichkeit) as the model to measure other men's work. Thus, he admired Fux's logical presentation of counterpoint in Gradus ad Parnassum and deplored Mattheson's rambling presentation of it in Capellmeister.[137] From his philosophical and literary pedigree, one would expect

Mizler to have supported the ideals of the German Enlightenment. From his admiration of Mattheson (on most points!) one would expect to find a love for the new, melodically oriented style. Even so, this was not the case. Mizler not only translated and admired Fux's treatise, a document of the stile antico, he also took the side of Bach in the Bach-Scheibe controversy. Perhaps Alfred Mann's comments about the Janus-like figure of Fux can be applied to Mizler as well.[138] His support of Bach and Fux places Mizler as a conservative from a musical-theoretical point of view, yet from a historical point of view his attitudes seem forward-looking. Certainly, his regard of Fux's work proved prophetic: it became the compositional bible for a string of composers from Haydn and Mozart to Richard Strauss.[139]

It seems certain that Mizler's interest in the stile antico was supported by his love for mathematical relationships and the arithmetic qualities of fugal composition. In this sense the polyphonic art of the high Baroque was better suited to Mizler's aesthetic outlook. It seems appropriate to mention Lewis White Beck's analogy between the philosophy of Leibniz, where certain ideas disappear only to reappear in different situations later on, and an enormous fugal composition, where a melodic theme threads its way through a series of intricate episodes.[140] The rigorous philosophical and mathematical constructs of the age of Leibniz and Wolff could never, in Mizler's eyes, find their musical corollaries in the musical style galant. That the counterpoint of Fux and Bach could, may help to explain Mizler's curious historical position, and why his contributions to musical thought are only now beginning to be appreciated.

1 Peter Smithers, The Life of Joseph Addison (Oxford: Clarendon Press, 1968), 45-90.

2 Ibid., 55.

3 Joseph Addison, "The Present State of the War and the Necessity of an Augmentation considered. 1707," in The Miscellaneous Works of Joseph Addison, ed. by A. C. Gutkelch (London: G. Bell & Sons, 1914), II, 241.

4 Smithers, Addison, 79.

5 Walter Graham, The Letters of Joseph Addison (Oxford: Clarendon Press, 1941), 3.

6 Smithers, Addison, 80.

7 Ibid., 80.

8 Ibid., 3, 80.

9 Ibid., 80.

10 See Renate Brockpähler, Handbuch zur Geschichte der Barockoper in Deutschland (Emsdetten: Verlag Lechte, 1964), 204; Walter Schulze, Die Quellen der Hamburger Oper (1678-1738) (Hamburg: Gerhard Stalling, 1938).

11 Brockpähler, Handbuch, 198.

12 Smithers, Addison, 79.

13 See Jane Randall, The Origins of the Scottish Enlightenment (London: Macmillan, 1978), 74-95; William T. Blackstone, Francis Hutcheson and Contemporary Ethical Theory (Athens, Georgia: University of Georgia Press, 1965); William Robert Scott, Francis Hutcheson: His Life, Teaching, and Position in the History of Philosophy (New York: Augustus M. Kelly, 1966).

14 Ernest Lee Tuveson, The Imagination as Means of Grace: Locke and the Aesthetics of Romanticism (Berkeley and Los Angeles: University of California Press, 1960), 123.

15 Scott, Hutcheson, 185.

16 Tuvenson, Imagination, 133.

17 Ibid., 134.

18 Monroe Beardsley, Aesthetics from Classical Greece to the Present (New York: Macmillan, 1966), 185.

19 Randall, Origins, 75.

20 Ibid., 75.

21 Scott, Hutcheson, 149.

22 Francis Hutcheson, An Inquiry Into the Original of our Ideas of Beauty and Virtue (2nd ed.; London, 1726), iv.

23 Peter Kivy, The Seventh Sense: A Study of Francis Hutcheson's Aesthetics and its Influence in Eighteenth-Century Britain (New York: Burt Franklin, 1976), 101.

24 Hutcheson, Inquiry, 25-26; additions and corrections to 1725 edition, 4-5.

25 Kivy, Seventh Sense, 250, 27n.

26 Both were sons of Protestant ministers, both lived for a time in Edinburgh, and both were admirers of Shaftesbury. Unfortunately, there is virtually no information available on Malcolm's early years.

27 Alexander Malcolm, A Treatise of Music: Speculative, Practical, and Historical (Edinburgh, 1721), 435.

28 Hutcheson, Inquiry, 6.

29 See Thomas Fowler, Shaftesbury and Hutcheson (New York: Putnam's Sons, 1883), 237; Hermann Hettner, Geschichte der englischen Literatur von der Wiederherstellung des Königthums bis in die zweite Hälfte des achtzehnten Jahrhunderts: 1660-1770 (5th ed.; Braunschweig: Vieweg, 1894).

30 See Frank Kidson, "Alexander Malcolm in America," Music and Letters, XXXIII (1952), 226-231.

31 Ibid., 228.

32 Henry George Farmer, _A History of Music in Scotland_ (London: Hinrichsen, 1947), 323.

33 Malcolm, _Treatise_, 384.

34 Ibid., 452.

35 Ibid., 474.

36 Ibid., see 60, 80, 178, and 312.

37 Ibid., 595.

38 Karl Darenberg, _Studien zur englischen Musikästhetik_ (Hamburg: Cram-de Gruyter, 1960), 49.

39 John Wilson, "North," in _New Grove's Dictionary_, 13, 286.

40 John Wilson, _Roger North on Music: Being a Selection from his Essays written during the years c.1695-1728_ (London: Novello, 1959), xix.

41 Jamie Croy Kassler, _The Science of Music in Britain, 1714-1830: A Catalogue of Writings, Lectures and Inventions_ (New York and London: Garland, 1979), 800.

42 See Michael Gillingham, "Bernhardt Schmidt," in _NGD_, 17, 41; William Leslie Sumner, _The Organ: its Evolution, Principles of Construction and Use_ (4th ed.; London: MacDonald and Jane's, 1973), 139-146; Andrew Freeman, _Father Smith otherwise Bernard Schmidt, being an Account of a Seventeenth-Century Organ Maker_ (London: At the Office of "Musical Opinion," 1926).

43 Wilson, _Roger North_, xviii.

44 Freeman, _Father Smith_, 6.

45 Sumner, _The Organ_, 142.

46 Ibid., 142.

47 This is number 70 in Freeman's catalogue of Smith organs.

48 Wilson, Roger North, 135.

49 Michael Tilmouth, "Prendcourt," in New Grove's Dictionary, 15, 214-215.

50 Wilson, Roger North, 55-56.

51 Ibid., 55.

52 Michael Tilmouth, "Finger," in New Grove's Dictionary, 6, 565-566.

53 Wilson, Roger North, 312.

54 Ibid., 354.

55 Ibid., 87; see also J. Merrill Knapp, "A Forgotten Chapter in English Eighteenth-Century Opera," Music and Letters, XLIII (1961), 4-16.

56 John Hawkins, A General History of the Science and Practice of Music (London, 1875 ed.), 724, 908.

57 Francis Espinasse, "James Ralph," in DNB, 16, 664-667. The question of whether or not Ralph was the actual author of the Touchstone was raised by Irving Lowens in "The Touchstone (1728): A Neglected View of London Opera," Musical Quarterly, XLV (1959), 325-342, and answered by John B. Shipley in "The Authorship of the Touchstone (1728)," in Papers of the Bibliographical Society of America, LXII (1968), 189-198. See also Ellen Harris, "An American Offers Advice to Handel," in American Choral Review, XXVII (1985), 55-62.

58 The Works of Benjamin Franklin, ed. by Jared Sparks (Boston: Hilliard Gray, 1840), I, 48.

59 The Poems of Henry Carey, ed. by Frederick T. Wood (London: Scholar's Press, 1930), 261.

60 Espinasse, "Ralph," 664.

61 See Malcolm Boyd, "Pepusch," in New Grove's Dictionary, 14, 357-360; Charles Cudworth, in MGG 10, 1026-1031; Lydia Miller Middleton, in DNB XV, 199-201.

62 Cudworth, "Pepusch," 1026.

63 Louis Fred Chenette, "Music Theory in the British Isles During the Enlightenment" (Ph.D. dissertation, Ohio State University, 1967).

64 Charles Burney, A General History of Music (New York: Dover, 1957), II, 987.

65 Ibid., II, 988.

66 Chenette, "Music Theory," 161.

67 Boyd, "Pepusch," 358.

68 John Christopher Pepusch, A Treatise of Harmony (London, 1731), 70.

69 Chenette, "Music Theory," 310; on Lampe see Dennis R. Martin, The Operas and Operatic Style of John Frederick Lampe (Detroit: Detroit Monographs in Musicology, Number 8, 1985); James Cuthbert Hadden, "Lampe," in DNB, XI, 470-471; Roger Fiske, "Lampe," in New Grove's Dictionary, 10, 419-421; and Charles Cudworth, "Lampe," in MGG, 8, 152-154.

70 Martin, Lampe, 3-19; Cudworth, "Lampe," 152.

71 Ibid., 152.

72 Hadden, "Lampe," 471.

73 John Frederick Lampe, A Plain and Comprehensive Method of Teaching Thorough Bass (London, 1737), vi.

74 John Frederick Lampe, The Art of Musick (London, 1740), 2.

75 Ibid., 20.

76 Chenette, "Music Theory," 67.

77 Lampe, Art, 4-5, 14.

78 Ibid., 44.

79 Chenette, "Music Theory," 320.

80 See Beekman C. Cannon, <u>Johann Mattheson: Spectator in Music</u> (New Haven: Yale University Press, 1947).

81 Ibid., 114-145.

82 Ibid., 115.

83 Johann Mattheson, <u>Das neu-eröffnete Orchestre</u> (Hamburg, 1713), 34.

84 Ibid., 2: "von den Dingen und Zeichen die zu einer musicalischen Composition gehören; von der musicalischen Composition und dem Contrapunct an sich selbst; wie eines und anders in der Music zu beurtheilen."

85 Cannon, <u>Mattheson</u>, 39.

86 George Buelow, "Mattheson," in <u>New Grove's Dictionary</u>, xx, 833.

87 Cannon, <u>Mattheson</u>, 37.

88 Ibid., 158.

89 Walter Graham, <u>The Beginnings of English Literary Periodicals: A Study of Periodical Literatue 1665-1715</u> (New York: Thomas Nelson, 1926), 84.

90 Cannon, <u>Mattheson</u>, 96-97.

91 The complete title is: <u>Das forschende Orchestre, oder desselben dritte Eröffnung, darinn Sensus Vindiciae et Quartae Blanditiae, das ist, der beschirmte Sinnen-Rang, und der schmeichelnde Quarten-Klang, allen unpartheyischen Syntechnitis, zum Nutzen und Nachdenken; keinem Menschen aber zum Nachtheil, sana ratione et autoritate untersuchet und vermuhtlich in ihr rechtes Licht gestellet worden von Johann Mattheson</u>.

92 Cannon, <u>Mattheson</u>, 62-90.

93 See Hugo Goldschmidt, <u>Die Musikästhetik des 18. Jahrhunderts</u> (Zurich and Leipzig: Rascher, 1915), 58-59; Cannon, <u>Mattheson</u>, 113n.

94 Mattheson, Forschende Orchestre, 186, 186n. This "oversight" was never corrected.

95 Mattheson, Critica Musica (Hamburg, 1722-1725), I, 250: Dieses ist bekannt, daß die Syllogismi, von verschiedenen Jahren her, (...) da sie doch das einzige Mittel zu Erfindung der Wahrheit bleiben.

96 Beck, Early German Philsophy, 267.

97 Mattheson, Der musikalische Patriot (Hamburg, 1728), 27. Wolff's original comments are taken from his Vernünftigen Gedancken von dem gesellschaftlichen Leben der Menschen und Insonderheit dem Gemeinen Wesen (4th ed.; Frankfurt and Leipzig: 1736), 385.
Wozu nützt es, wenn in der Wolffischen Politic p. 385 also geschrieben stehet: "Zur Ergetzlichkeit der Ohren gehört die Music, so wol die Instrumental- als Vocal-Music, oder das Singen:" Ein jeder, der nie was von Wissenschafften gehöret hat, urtheilet fast eben so künstlich; aber das weiß ein jeder nicht, daß die Music zur Seelen- und Tugend-Erbauung gehöret. So mögte billig ein Politicus und Philosophos reden was hat der eigentlich mit den Ohren zu schaffen? Weiter meldet der berühmte Wolff: "Man habe in dieser Absicht im gemein Wesen auch Musicanten von nöthen, die bey sich eräugenden Fällen, durch das Ohr ein Vergnügen machen konnen." Das ist aber ein sehr kriechende, und nicht die wahre Absicht der Music, in so fern sie dem gemeinen Wesen nützen soll; dadurch wird ja allen Bierfiedlern das Wort geredet.
Herr Wolff meldet ferner: "Man wisse aus der Erfahrung, daß im Gedächtnisse nichts besser bleibe, als abgesungene Verse, und daß die Music geschickt sey, allerley Arten der Affecten zu erregen, welche die Regeln der Tugenden und anständigen Sitten mit sich verknüpfen etc." Thut denn da die Music nichts mehr, als dass sie die Ohren ergetzet? Der Herr Autor rühmt sich sonst seiner Schreib-Art, und setzt verschiedene mahl: "Nach meiner Art, nach meiner Art," d. i. (wie er selbst auslegt) "deutlich und gründlich." Wer ein Exempel davon haben will, lese seine Worte p. 85. wo es so heißt: "Es ist öffters mehr daran gelegen, daß Eltern Kinder Geld erwerben und damit recht umgehen lernen," etc. Denn, zu geschwiegen, daß allezeit, und nicht nur äffters, daran gelegen ist, so sollte es ja billig hier heissen: "Daß Eltern die Kinder lehren (nicht lernen) wie sie Geld erwerben, und damit recht umgehen mögen." Diese wenige beiläuffig, als ein Muster der Deutlichkeit.

Was weiter l. c. vom Misbrauch der Music vorgebracht, auch wolbedächtlich mit "Geilheit, Üppigkeit" etc. starck bespickt wird, ist das alte Endlose Lied. Und mein! thut der gute, hochgeehrte Wolff mit obigem Antrage der Music wol die geringste Ehre, da er vorher p. 384. die Beflissene derselben, die Opernisten, die wahren Academicos musicos (exceptis excipiendis) mit den liederlichsten Taschen-Spielern richtig in eine Classe, und noch ein grosses et cetera dazu gesetzet hatte?

98 Wolff, Vernünfftige Gedancken, 385.

99 Mattheson, Critica musica, I, 313: Ein Schottländischer Autor, Malcolm genannt, hat ein Capitel davon geschrieben, und zwar auf meine Veranlassung, gestalten ich etliche Jahr her mit ihm dieserwegen in correspondence stehe.

100 Ibid., I, 146-147.

101 Mattheson, Forschendes Orchestre, 725-726: Wie könne man wissen ob uns der Tag lieblich wäre, wenn nicht die unangenehme, und doch erträglich-finstere Nacht dazwischen käme. (...) Wenn aber der Dissonanzen mehr sind, als der Consonanzen, und jene auch länger dauern, als diese, dabey nicht einmahl resolviret werden, so ist es schon verdriesslich, und wieder die Natur.

102 Ibid., 728: Die Dissonanzen wären die Finsterniß (ich möchte lieber sagen: der Schatten) die Consonanzen das Licht. Das Licht wurde uns so angenehm nicht seyn, wenn es immer Tag, und niemahls Nacht wäre.

103 Johann Mattheson, Der vollkommene Capellmeister, trans. by Ernest C. Harriss (Ann Arbor: UMI Research Press, 1981), 569-570.

104 Cannon, Mattheson, 81-82.

105 Ibid., 193-194.

106 Ibid., 87.

107 Johann Mattheson, Der vollkommene Capellmeister (Hamburg, 1738), 9-10; trans. by Ernest C. Harriss, (Ann Arbor: UMI Research Press, 1981), 36.

108 Scheibe, Critischer Musicus, 40, 375-376.

109 Scheibe, Critischer Musicus, 2nd ed., 4-5.

110 Wöhlke, Mizler, 95; Federhofer, "Fux und Mattheson," 119-123.

111 Mattheson-Harris, Capellmeister, 110; Mattheson, Capellmeister, 19.

112 Ibid., 112; 21.

113 Ibid., 688, 880n; 363, 363n.

114 Gustav Adoph Seibel, Das Leben des königl. Polnischen und kurfürstl. Sächs. Hofkapellmeisters Johann David Heinichen nebst chronologischem Verzeichnis seiner Opern (Leipzig: Brietkopf & Härtel, 1913), 11.

115 Johann David Heinichen, Neu-erfundene und gründliche Anweisung (Hamburg, 1711).

116 Johann Mattheson, Das beschützte Orchestre (Hamburg, 1717).

117 Johann David Heinichen, Der General-Baß in der Composition (Dresden, 1728), 838-839.

118 Johann Mattheson, Große Generalbaßschule (Hamburg, 1731), 10.

119 Heinichen, General-Baß, 18n-19n: Alle Künste und Wissenschaften haben ihre Regeln, und müssen durch Regeln erlernet werden, wofern wir nicht pure Naturalisten, das ist, halbe Ignoranten bleiben wollen. Allein wir müssen nur nicht in excessu unnützer Regeln pecciren; viel weniger müssen wir das aequivoque Wort: Regeln so barbare annehmen, als wolten wir hochtrabende Regel-Schmiede abgeben, und der Natur selbst Gesätze vorschreiben, (...) Nein! alle unsers nutzbare Regeln müssen vorhero aus der Natur selbst genommen, und dieser Herscherin ihr Wille, Neigung, und Eigneschafft nach allen Gradibus erforschet, und ihr gleichsam cum submissione abgemercket werden: aus diesen Observationibus aber nehmen wir erst unsere Regeln.

120 Seibel, Heinichen, 8-9.

121 Beck, <u>Early German Philosphy</u>, 256-257.

122 Baron, <u>Study</u>, 8-9; Baron, <u>Untersuchung</u>, 9: Und warum solte es nicht angehen die gantze Music in mehere Deutlichkeit zu bringen, als man es mit der Philosophie würcklich zu Stande gebracht. Wem sind nicht des erlauchten Herrn von Leibnitz, des vortrefflichen geheimen Rath Thomasii, und des hochberühmten Hof-Rath Wolffens Schrifften bekannt? welcher letztere alle metaphysische so genannte Kunst-Wörter und Excorcistereyen derer Schul Geister so gefährlich sie immer geklungen, in das schönste hoch-teutsche übersetzt. Geht es nun in solchen Dingen an, die man sonst vor unglaublich gehalten, warum solte dieses nicht auch in der Music angehen?

123 Baron, <u>Study</u>, vii-ix.

124 Birke, <u>Wolff</u>, 91-96.

125 Ibid., 92: Zur Schöpfung einer guten Melodie wird erfordert
1. ein gut Naturell welches
a) in einem guten Verstande bestehet, nehmlich in dem Vermögen, sich alles was in der Musik möglich ist, deutlich vorzustellen.
b) auch in Witz, der ist eine Fertigkeit, die Ähnlichkeiten warzunehmen, und wer solchen besitzt, ist sinnreich und zu allerhand Erfindungen geschickt.
c) auch Einbildungskraft, welche eine Kraft der Seele, sich Melodien und deren Einrichtung leicht vorzustellen.
d) auch Beurtheilungskraft, durch welche man unterscheidet, was einer Sache zukommt und was ihr nicht zukommt, was ihr eigen und nicht eigen, und wie sie von andern Dingen unterschieden ist.
2. Die Cultur, welche geschehen muss
*) durch das Clavier, weil dieses die ganze Harmonie in sich begreifft, darauf man
1. mit kleinen Melodien anfangen muss, und dann
2. mit grössern stuffenweise fortfahren, um Ideen von Melodien zu kriegen, und dan wird
3. der Generalbass zum Grunde gesetzt, durch welche man die
a. Consonantien und
b. die Dissonantien, auch deren Gebrauch und folglich
c. die völlige Harmonie kennen lernt.
*) Die Übung. Denn wenn einer anfängt Melodien zu erfinden; so muss er solches erst mit kleinen Galanterie-Stücken

probiren, bis er nach und nach zu höherer Wissenschaft gelanget, dabey er in Acht zu nehmen hat
1. Die Erkänntniss der Modorum,
2. Ihrer Leibsemitonen
3. Ihrer Ausschweifungen und
4. Die unvermerkte Art wieder in Modum zu kommen.

126 Baron, Study, 161; Baron, Untersuchung, 191: ...am leichtesten, deutlichsten und vollständigsten vor vielen andern geschrieben.

127 Immanuel Wilheim, "J. A. Scheibe: German Musical Thought in Transition" (Ph.D. dissertation, University of Illinois, 1963); G. J. Skapski, "The Recitative in J. A. Scheibe's Literary and Musical Work" (Ph.D. dissertation, University of Texas, 1963); Peter Benary, Die deutsche Kompositionslehre des 18. Jahrhunderts (Leipzig: Breitkopf & Härtel, 1961).

128 George Buelow, "Scheibe," in New Grove's Dictionary, 16, 599-600.

129 See Hans Gunther Hoke, "Mizler," in MGG, 6, 388-392; George Buelow, "Mizler," in New Grove's Dictionary, 12, 372-373; and Franz Wöhlke, Lorenz Christoph Mizler (Würzburg: Konrad Triltsch, 1940).

130 Buelow, "Mizler," 372.

131 Wöhlke, Mizler, 38.

132 See Alfred Mann's introduction to his edition of Fux's Gradus ad Parnassum (Kassel and Graz: Bärenreiter, 1967); Hellmut Federhofer, "Johann Josef Fux und Johann Mattheson im Urteil Lorenz Christoph Mizlers," in Festgabe für Heinrich Husmann, ed. by H. Becker and R. Gerlach (Munich: Wilhelm Fink, 1970), 111-123.

133 See Chapter I of this study.

134 Lorenz Mizler, Die neu-eröffnete musicalische Bibliothek (Leipzig, 1736-1754), I, iv, 7, 75-75n: Den Nutzen der Wolfischen Weltweisheit in der Musik werde ich in einer besondern Schrift: de usu ac praestantis philosophiae Wolfianae in musicae, zeigen.

135 Birke, Wolff, 68.

136 Flaherty, *Opera*, 126.

137 Federhofer, "Fux und Mattheson," 119.

138 Mann, *Gradus*, xiv.

139 Ibid., xviii-xix.

140 Beck, *Early German Philosophy*, 203.

CHAPTER IV

THE AFFECTIONS: BIRTH AND DEATH OF A CONCEPT

The concept of the affections had an important place in writings on all the arts, not just those on music, during the early eighteenth century. It was a rare treatise indeed which had no section dealing with any of several aspects of this ancient concept, be it a text on poetics or gardening. Even so, a noticeable decrease in the confidence of writers on music in the validity of the affective theory can be seen during the first four decades of the eighteenth century. In the 1720s Alexander Malcolm questioned the necessity of the concept itself, and by the 1730s most writers attempted to relate the affections to their own special viewpoints. Thus, Mattheson's dicussion of the affections in _Capellmeister_ actually focus on melody, Mizler's on science. These shifts of emphasis were manifestations of the gradual realization that the concept of the affections had outlived its usefulness.

It should be remembered that the "doctrine" of affections was from the outset no system, but a collection of ideas and formulas which varied as its users varied. This, coupled with the tendency of modern writers to view the concept as some sort of standardized code, has given rise to considerable confusion about it. Donald Jay Grout, for example, speaks of "a systematic, regulated vocabulary, a common repertory of musical figures or devices."[1] This attitude is occasionally combined with a lack of appreciation for the rhetorical roots of the concept of the affections and its sister doctrine (as Hans Lenneberg has called it), rhetoric, though this problem has been successfully dealt with in the writings of George Buelow.[2] The following presentation can be seen as an introduction to a new appreciation of the concept of the affections itself, based on the work of Lenneberg and Buelow. The theories and attitudes discussed here will be further developed when we examine actual writings on music.

An Unsystematic System: Ancient Thought on the Affections

The beginnings of the concept of affections are to be found not in philosophical writings per se, but in ancient medical treatises. The concept of the four temperaments, for example, was presented in the writings of Hippocrates. Here good health is regarded as a balance of four qualities --cold, hot, wet, and dry. These qualities are also represented by the four seasons and, in general, Hippocrates regarded the external environment as the determining factor in healthiness. It was the somewhat later physician, Galen, who provided a more complex system, in which the humors (yellow and black bile, blood, and phlegm) could be blended in varying proportions--the result being good or ill health.[3] As important as these medical writings are, however, the affections were an important part of the religious life of the ancient Greeks. Music was often united with dance during the initiations of followers of Dionysus, for example, and their "imitation" (dance-pantomime) of the God was manifested by a frenzy which symbolized the mystical presence of God in man. Thus, the imitation of the God himself resulted in the raising of the affection of transcendent intoxication which was in itself a type of spiritual purgative.[4]

The concept of affections grew to the extent that the raising or re-creation of them became the common denominator between all the arts, including music. Simply stated, the artist would imitate the desired affection and the audience would then experience it as well. Thus the affection itself was something more than just a sensation. It was a collection of several factors--the universal affection, the created affection, the apprehended affection--which form a single affective unity.[5] Early on, the connection between music and soul was recognized in discussions dealing with education. Specific affective connotations were assigned to certain modes, for example, or melodic inflections.[6] The most famous discussions of music by both Plato (Republic) and Aristotle (Politics) deal with this ethical quality of music.[7] Even before Plato or Aristotle, however, the affective quality of music was recognized--not only by medical authorities, but, as we have already seen, in the mythic-spiritual world of Greek religious practice.[8]

During the next several centuries Greek thought on the affections was refined and modified. These refinements sometimes took the form of attempts to deal with specific, identifiable methods of raising affections. Sometimes attitudes toward the affections represented the basic philosophical attitude of a given school of thinkers. This was the case with Epicurean writers, who divided the affections into two large areas--those of pain and those of pleasure.[9] The pleasure-oriented philosophy of Epicurus is by its nature empirical, and Lucretius' De rerum Natura contains several examples of specific affective association.[10] Probably the most important ancient writer on the affections, for our purposes, was Marcus Fabius Quintilianus, or Quintilian (AD 30-?). His Institutio oratoria became one of the main sources of information on the affections for writers in the Baroque and early eighteenth century.[11] Quintilian held music in high regard, and included it as part of the training for young orators. Even though he was most interested in the spoken word as the form most appropriate for ethic presentations, he did imply the same ethic power to music. Quintilian's text, and its implicit recognition of the ties between music and rhetoric, provided an important basis for the later connections between the two arts developed during later centuries, particularly the eighteenth.[12]

Attitudes Toward the Affections in the Early Eighteenth Century

As we have already seen in Chapter I, the concept of the affections was often discussed during the two centuries previous to the eighteenth. The affections were also of importance when related to the systems of rhetoric, particularly as taught in the Lateinschulen of northern Germany. In musical texts the relation of the affections with musical rhetoric is so pronounced that the difference between the two is blurred. The early eighteenth century witnessed the high-water mark of influence for the concept, and it was at that time, especially in German writings, that the empirical attempts flourished to codify the affections' qualities by establishing a systematized

Figurenlehre. In so doing, German musicians continued the trend set over one hundred years earlier by Kircher. The first three decades of the eighteenth century were rich in enumerations of musico-rhetorical figures. Arnold Schmitz has pointed out in his study of musical figures that even later writers (J. A. Scheibe, for example) believed that, while music might move listeners without these figures, it was not possible to raise specific affections without them.[13]

Another aspect of the concept of the affections which most eighteenth-century discussions share is a view of the universe divided into realms of sensual experience and rational (reasoning) experience. Similarly, the relationship between the concept of the affections and the ars rhetorica necessitated the throwing together of rationalistic a priori attitudes with empirical ones, resulting in a kind of mixture of concepts and ideas which was common in the eighteenth century. Thus, Johann Mattheson could rest his theories about the affections on the shoulders of Descartes (which he does explicitly in Der vollkommene Capellmeister), the so-called father of rationalism, and could elsewhere translate page after page of John Locke's Of Human Understanding for inclusion in Das forschende Orchestre. Although Beekman Cannon has pointed out the importance of Locke's influence on Mattheson, Appendix II of this study lists all the references to Locke by Mattheson in Das forschende Orchestre.[14] Mattheson saw no rationalistic-empirical dilemma here, and we should avoid attempting to separate writers on music into rationalistic and empirical camps. It is just as problematic to regard a certain writer as baroque if he acknowledges the validity of the concept of the affections, and another as pre-classical because he does not.

Certainly, conservative writers dealt more expansively with the affections, and more progressive thinkers (Addison, for example) passed over the concept rather quickly. Yet, even the lengthy discussions of the affections by German writers in the 1730s reflect less of an interest in the concept than in some newer aesthetic issue, such as melodic writing or musical texture.

Addison and Mattheson: Views on the Concept of the Affections in the First Two Decades of the Eighteenth Century

In *Spectator* No. 29 (April 3, 1711) Addison discusses the problems of "Tone or Accent" which recitative raises, noting the difference between the speech habits in Scotland and Wales:

> For this Reason, the Recitative Musick in every Language should be as different as the Tone or Accent of each Language, for otherwise what may properly express a Passion in one Language, will not do it in another. 15

The passing reference here to the affections is, unfortunately, typical: there is no thorough discussion of the passions in either the *Tatler* or *Spectator*. Even so, one can at least say that Addison was aware of the concept and regarded the expression of a given passion as one of music's important functions. If it did not succeed in this it was somehow faulty. As a conclusion to this first part of his essay Addison attempts metaphorically to present the place of Italian music in Britain. English birds, we are told, "mellow the Harshness of their natural Notes by practising under those that come from warmer climates."[16] Similarly, British musicians should not avoid Italian influences, but rather allow themselves to be polished by it. Addison concludes with a warning: "Let the Infusion be as strong as you please, but still let the Subject Matter of it be English."[17]

Unlike Addison, Johann Mattheson was intriqued with the concept of the affections his entire life. Beekman Cannon described him as "the most prominent representative of the Cartesian doctrine of "affections" in music."[18] Although Das neu-eröffnete Orchestre treats the affections less thoroughly than his later works, Mattheson does comment on the affective characteristics of each key. Mattheson begins by noting that everyone knows that each scale has certain characteristics and type of effect on the listener.[19] He agrees with those who find the third scale degree of critical importance, but this alone is hardly sufficient to explain the variety of affections possible to produce. Mattheson concludes his twenty-page discussion of keys and affections with this paragraph:

> The little which has been communicated here on the character of each key to the curious could lead to a very large discussion. If everything which one could say or think was added, every key would fill a chapter of its own. The more laws one would seek to legislate, the more contradictions would probably be found. [The reason] that the flood of opinions is almost numberless I can only explain by the difference between human complexions--which is without doubt the major cause that a key which seems lively and encouraging to a sanguine temperament may seem full of care, woeful, and depressed to a phlegmatic, and so on. Therefore, we will not linger here any longer, but gladly leave to each the freedom to attribute to one or another key the properties which most agree with his natural inclinations. 20

Mattheson was a realist. Like Addison, he admits the problem of varying inclinations within a given audience. Still, he does not comment on the ramifications of this fact on the concept--ignoring the paradox like many writers of his century. The fundamental distinction between the rationalistic basis of the concept of the affections and the empirical proofs against it was not the question. Differences between not just nations but individuals were recognized, but the conclusions which seem obvious to a twentieth-century observer were not reached by the eighteenth-century mind.

The Concept of the Affections in the 1720s

The following quotation from Alexander Malcolm's treatise presents his conception of the affections fairly well:

> This Species [i.e., type of music] is by some called particularly the Mundane Musick. 3d. Human, which consists chiefly in the Harmony of the Faculties of the human Soul, and its various Passions; and is also considered in the Proportion and Temperament, mutual Dependence and Connection, of all the Parts of this wonderful Machine of our Bodies. 4th. Is what in a more limited and peculiar Sense of the Word was called Musick; which has for its object Motion, considered as under certain regular measures and Proportions, by which it affects the senses in an agreeable manner. 21

Though possessing considerable knowledge of the concept, Malcolm did have reservations. He regarded the concept of modes as capable of creating specific emotive states as absurd. His discussion supporting the music of the moderns over that of the ancients notes that modern music makes use of instruments--and often only instruments. The purpose of this music, he points out, "is not so much to move the Passions, as to entertain the Mind and please the Fancy."[22] He later comments:

> But why must the moving of particular Passions be the only Use of Musick? If we look upon a noble Building, or a curious Painting, we are allowed to admire the Design, and view all its Proportions and Relations in Parts with Pleasure to our Understandings, without any respect to the Passions. We must observe again, that there is scarce any Piece of Melody that has not some general influence upon the Heart; and by being more sprightly or heavy in its Movements, will have different Effects; tho' it is not designed to excite any particular Passion, and can only be said in general to give Pleasure and recreate the Mind. 23

We will return to this passage when we discuss the imagination in Malcolm's work. As these last passages show, Malcolm acknowledged the concept of the affections but felt music was a force which extended beyond it. Long before Charles Avison, a British writer on music seized upon a new and fruitful aspect of musical thought--the use of music for something more than just raising passions.[24]

Roger North, a more conservative writer, makes it clear in his "Essay of Musicall Ayre" that a discussion of the passions is a "most difficult subject."[25] Perhaps because of this he limits his remarks on the topic in his "Essay" to a brief reference to the relationship between affections and keys.[26] In his Musical Grammarian North discusses the topic more fully, pointing out the correlation between composers and other creative artists who must use their powers of imagination to conceive larger projects before actually beginning them. These thoughts must, we are told, give unity to the diverse imaginings of the artist. North cites the famous "Pest House" of Raphael and asks who would not be moved by it. He then asks the reader to imagine a musical work composed to fit the picture. Surely, North argues, the musician's internal state would have to be similar to that of Raphael when he painted the work. A musician must, if he is to move his audience, possess an idea of the passion he wished to present before he begins the compositional process.[27] North also provides a guide to the various states which music can represent:

> These are sedate griefs; but the utterances of extream pain, torture, or fright in any creature can never be represented in musick, for they are always the worst of discord. But the extreams of joy and happyness are commonly exprest in the sharp keys, imitating trumpetts and merry songs usuall on such occasions; and all the dancing, theatricall, and festivous musick is chiefly of that kind. 28

James Ralph's attitude toward the concept of the affections is also uncritical. Interestingly, Ralph, who professes that poetry is the highest form of art, makes several surprisingly strong statements about music's ability to raise the passions, "to touch the different Passions, as justly as any kind of Poetry."[29] Ralph also admits that "touching and, of consequence, improving the Passions, is the highest Flight that Art, in conjunction with Nature, can soar."[30] What is most important about Ralph's use of this term is his infrequent use of it. Much more interested in discussing social events in London, Ralph never philosophized in depth on the subject. Like North, Malcolm, and most British writers of the early eighteenth century, Ralph was satisfied to avoid detailed discussions of the affections.

Mattheson's attitude toward the affections is reevaluated in the 1720s. Das forschende Orchestre examines the concept in the context of sense and sense experience, whereas the discussion in Critica Musica reflects Mattheson's preoccupation with melody at that time. The discussion in Das forschende Orchestre begins with an examination of the sense of hearing, Mattheson calling it the most powerful of all the senses since "through hearing, the mind and its affections are most powerfully aroused."[31] This remark is supported by statements paraphrased from Locke, who noted that the sense of hearing offered "the most immediate entry into the spirit of man."[32]

Mattheson's discussion of the affections in _Critica Musica_ is even more detailed. To Mattheson, the melody was the carrier of affections and excessive counterpoint lessened affective impact. Commenting on Bokemeyer's defense of dense polyphonic writing, Mattheson observes that the combination of four or more melodies "confuse, darken, glue-up the main point, the main modulation, and the affection."[33] Mattheson expands his discussion of the affections in a defense of instrumental music, noting that "no _grammaticus_, no speaker, can speak or write as can the tones," that is, instrumental music can express the passions better than the spoken word.[34]

Johann David Heinichen's attitude toward the concept of the affections was bound up with his ideas about classical rhetoric, a fact best illustrated by his long discussion of the _loci topici_ or _sedes argumentuum_ (sources of arguments) as Quintilian called them.[35] Even so, Heinichen's use of the idea of _loci topici_ shows less a desire to bring rhetorical arts into the creative act than to intellectualize simple matter of common sense. This represents one of his chief differences from Mattheson. For Heinichen, intellectualization of his art seems to have been more a duty than a pleasure, whereas Mattheson had no difficulty in writing many pages of highly philosophical prose, Heinichen seemed anxious to get to more of the practical matters at hand as soon as possible.

Heinichen presents the *loci topici* in the context of the imagination. How, he asks, can a composer write an aria on an uninspiring text?

> To direct our thoughts to good ideas, however, and to encourage natural fantasy can best be accomplished, in my opinion, by use of the oratorical *Locos Topicos*. 36

Heinichen describes three main types of *loci topici*: *antecedentia textus*, *concomitantia textus*, and *consequentia textus*. Formulating these categories is, however, a long-winded way of instructing the composer to a) look at the text before the section to be set to music to discover any new and inspiring meanings b) choose one particular word in the text which offers possibilities for the composer, or c) look at the text following the section to be actually set, again to find some kind of hint at how the previous text should be handled. Heinichen simply tells the composer to read the entire libretto, not just the sections set as arias, or to decide on a particularly emotion-laden word and focus on that. Heinichen's combined use of the concept of the affections and rhetoric is characteristic for German writers of his generation. The musical *inventio* and the *loci topici* are important factors in Heinichen's musical universe and reflect his attitude "that our *finis musices* is to move the affections."[37]

Less philosophical about the affections than Mattheson, and less explicit than Heinichen, Ernst Gottlieb Baron revealed some skepticism toward the concept. This is best seen in his discussion on the effects of the passions where he makes this note about the stories of Kircher and other earlier writers, who maintained that music was capable of driving men insane: "Those who tell such stories lived during times when more fables than truths were heard, and the whole matter is not as serious as has been asserted."[38] For Baron it was not the music, but the natural inclination of the listener which resulted in such responses.

With his contemporaries Baron shared an interest in rhetoric. In his discussion "Genius on the Lute" in the Untersuchung, for example, he presents two styles of lute playing. The first, we are told, involves merely playing the notes as they are written down, without ornamentation. Baron considered musicians of this orientation lowly, not fit for playing at court. The other style, which Baron calls "oratorical", follows the example of the speaker, who is able to move his audience with his elegance of speech and the sublimity of his thoughts: "A virtuoso musician must possess all of these qualities."[39] Even so, Baron was not fond of rules, having found that "the rules of art are weak means with which we come to the aid of our corrupted souls."[40] For such a writer the most important aspect of music was sensual, and his empirical leanings ruled out elaborate discussions of the affections. Baron's simple observation, that all men had ears, but not all were moved in the same manner, was a manifestation of a basic discomfort with the concept of the affections, a discomfort which he shared with a growing number of writers.

The Concept of the Affections in the 1730s

It is impossible to examine Pepusch's views on the four terms selected for examination in this study since his treatise focuses on more prosaic matters of music making.

His discussion of the affections (the only one of the four aesthetic terms this study focuses on which he examines) illustrates this taciturnity. He makes no attempt to categorize or even label the affections. Considering his interest in Greek music, this seems remarkable. Certainly, one wishes Pepusch would have expanded on his remark that the major third is "chearful and sprightly ascending, but is the contrary descending; the minor [third] is the reverse, for it is sprightly descending but soft and tender ascending."[41] Pepusch makes no attempt to present information regarding the affective qualities of other intervals. Of rhetoric and music there is only the following comment on cadences:

> Cadences in Musick, are the same as Stops in Speaking, or in Writing; that is to say, They are Endings or Terminations either of a Part, or of the whole Piece of Musick; as stops are of a Part or of the whole Speech. 42

From the shortness of this and other discussions one assumes that Pepusch was less fascinated by the relationships between music and rhetoric than the theorists in his native land and that he was perhaps sensitive to the lack of interest in such matters in Britain.

John Frederick Lampe does not disavow the importance of concepts of the affections, though he is also vague in his discussion of it. One of the important aspects of the musical art, we are told in The Art of Musick, is an understanding of the importance of touching the passions. Without doing this no composer, however skilled in harmonic practices, will rise above the mediocre. His work, Lampe maintains, "most probably will be dull, flat, and insipid."[43] In presenting the major reasons for writing The Art of Musick, Lampe cites his desire to clarify music enough so that listeners will have some idea why their passions are so easily moved by it, and why "they find themselves touched."[44] Lampe's explanation never materialized, however, and his attempts to explain the effect of music on its listeners deals less with the realm of the affections than other aesthetic concepts, such as imitation and taste.

In Germany discussion of the affections reflected each writer's aesthetic bias. Few areas of inquiry interested Scheibe, for example, more than those concerning the relationship between music and rhetoric. With Gottsched's Critische Dichtkunst as his inspiration, Scheibe attempted to look at the affections in a new manner--though this may not seem immediately apparent.[45] Certainly his remark that the primary goal of music was to move the passions is nothing new.[46] His discussion of rhetorical figures and their musical counterparts are not far removed from Mattheson's or Heinichen's remarks in the twenties.[47] What is original in Scheibe's attitude is his desire to fit the concept of the affections into a larger scheme based on the laws of rhetoric, nature, and taste:

> So much is certain, that the closer we seek to come in music to the rules of rhetoric and poetics, the more certainly we will reach rationality and nature: and the more we trouble ourselves to discover what is beautiful or exceptional in a speech or a poem, the closer we will come to good taste in music, which up to now was unknown to almost all who understand something of music. 48

Scheibe was aware of the novelty of his position. Unlike Mattheson, whose approach to the affections was comparatively limited, Scheibe--as a good Wolffian--was conscious of the need for some kind of tangible connection between taste, nature, and rhetoric.

In his study of Scheibe, Immanuel Wilheim contends that "we look in vain for any trace of Affectenlehre [in Scheibe]" and points to Scheibe's unwillingness to discuss the affections in a specific manner and his advocacy of the concept of feeling (Empfindung).[49] While it seems fair to emphasize this interest in the concept of feeling, Wilheim's attempt to downplay the importance of the affections in Scheibe's work is not convincing. This is caused, in part, by Wilheim's decision to arbitrarily separate Scheibe's discussion of musical figures from the concept of the affections.[50] Since the concept of the affections is an integral part of the system of classical rhetoric which Scheibe attempted to emulate in music, his faith in the process of emotional response implied in the concept was strong. Scheibe is clear about this connection, noting that "figures are themselves a language of the affections, as Professor Gottsched in his Critische Dichtkunst, quoting the famous P. Lami, notes at length."[51] Wilheim's contention that "Scheibe, in fact, rather carefully sidesteps the question of expression of affections and passions in instrumental music," is also unjustified, as this quote from the Critischer Musicus shows:

> His [i.e., the composer's] melodies must move and take in the listener even without words. And so he must posses all the passions and emotions in his full power, and always be able to awake a new awareness [in his listeners]. 52

Like Scheibe, Lorenz Mizler used the concept of the affections for his own purposes. Mizler's goal was the "scientific," well illustrated by his criticisms of writers who ascribed emotional characteristics to certain keys (one thinks immediately of Mattheson's Das neu-eröffnete Orchestre). "Though it is certain," Mizler noted "that all major keys sound bright and cheery, and all minor keys sound properly comfortable and sad," one cannot go further.[53] The reason why a difference between major and minor keys could be made, according to Mizler, was related to the mathematically demonstrable difference between the major and minor third--each of which impacted upon the senses differently. Differences between the keys, however, were not mathematically demonstrable and therefore unworthy of discussion.

Mizler's admiration for Gottsched, together with his own training in rhetoric, caused references to relationships between music and literature to be common in his works. Both arts, he noted, had the same goal--to move the passions--and therefore the same rules and principles applied to both.[54] This recognition did not prevent Mizler from criticizing comparisons between music and rhetoric he found extreme, specifically the analysis of an aria by Benedetto Marcello found in Mattheson's Capellmeister.[55] Mattheson divided the aria into six parts, corresponding to the exordium, narratio, propositio, confirmatio, confutatio, and the peroratio of rhetoric. Mizler considered this analysis absurd, and suggested (characteristically enough) that composers would be better served if they studied the geometrical relationships between the sections of their works instead.[56]

Mizler's most extensive comments on the concept of the affections are found in his footnotes to the opera essays by Gottsched ("Thoughts on Opera") and Christoph Ludwig ("Attempt at a Proof, that a Singspiel or Opera cannot be Good").[57] Gottsched and Ludwig opposed opera since, in their opinion, it was unable to arouse or quiet the passions in a systematic manner. Ludwig, for example, noted that even if an aria did succeed in arousing the passions, the effect was lost when the recitative returned.[58] Even worse, Ludwig said, was the practice of employing two or more affections in the course of a single aria.[59] Mizler's response to such criticisms was always the same: the good composer avoided such pitfalls. In Mizler's view, opera could not be faulted simply because composers were inexpert.[60] It is significant that Mizler, unlike Malcolm, did not attempt to refute the premise that music must move the passions. Mizler had no desire to abandon a system which in its various manifestations had served the arts well for almost two thousand years. He no doubt felt that, if it was admitted that music did not raise the passions, a logical conclusion would be that music was indeed a mere "amusement for the ear."

What was new in Mattheson's discussions of the affections in the 1730s (and different from Scheibe and Mizler) was the amount of space given to the relationship between the affections and melody. Even so, Mattheson does follow the pattern of writers in the 1730s who unite the concept of the affections with their major interests. The idea that melody was the primary "carrier" of the affections was prepared by earlier statements, but in Capellmeister Mattheson was more clear, noting that "the stirring of the affections and passions of the soul depends on something quite different, namely upon the skillful composition of an intelligible, clear, and expressive melody."[61] Mattheson also saw a link between the theory of the passions and the science of melody.[62] One other interesting aspect of Mattheson's _Capellmeister_ should be mentioned. Commenting on the relationship between recitative and affection, he noted that one could extend the discussion of affective disposition of an audience "to entire cultures, to which one can, to a certain measure, attribute a pervasive temperament."[63] These remarks are, of course, very similar to Addison's in _Spectator_ No. 29, and may have also been the source of Scheibe's interest in that particular topic.

1 Donald J. Grout, A History of Western Music (3rd ed.; New York: Norton, 1973), 299.

2 Hans Lenneberg, "Johann Mattheson on Affects and Rhetoric in Music," Journal of Music Theory, II (1958), 47; George Buelow, "Johann Mattheson and the invention of the Affektenlehre," in New Mattheson Studies, ed. by George Buelow and Hans Joachim Marx, (Cambridge: Cambridge University Press, 1983), 393-407.

3 See Galen, On the Usefulness of the Parts of the Body, trans. by Margaret Tallmadge May (Ithaca: Cornell University Press, 1968), I, 45.

4 See S. H. Butcher, Aristotle's Theory of Poetry and Fine Arts (New York: Dover, 1951), 121ff.

5 Annemarie Jeanette Neubecker, Altgriechische Musik (Darmstadt: Wissenschaftliche Buchgesellschaft, 1977), 127-130.

6 D. B. Monro, The Modes of Ancient Greek Music (Oxford: Clarendon Press, 1894), 7-9, 12-15.

7 Edward H. Lippman. Musical Thought in Ancient Greece (New York: Columbia, 46-47.

8 See James Frazer, The Golden Bough: A Study in Magic and Religion, (3rd ed.; New York: Macmillan, 1935), 54-55.

9 Walter Serauky, Die musikalische Nachahmungsästhetik im Zeitraum von 1700 bis 1759 (Münster: Helios, 1929), 4.

10 V. Cauchy, "Epicureanism," in The New Catholic Encyclopedia (New York: McGraw-Hill, 1967), V, 466-468.

11 George Buelow, "Musical Rhetoric," in New Grove's Dictionary, XV, 801.

12 See Hans-Heinrich Unger, Die Beziehung zwischen Musik und Rhetorik im 16.-18. Jahrhundert (Würzburg: Konrad Triltsch, 1942), 12.

13 Arnold Schmitz, "Die oratorische Kunst J. S. Bachs --Grundfragen und Grundlagen," in Gesellschaft für Musikforschung Kongreß-Bericht Lüneburg (Kassel: Bärenreiter, 1950), 33-49.

14 Beekman Cannon, Johann Mattheson: Spectator in Music (New Haven: Yale University Press, 1947), 85, 117-118, 121-122.

15 Joseph Addison and Richard Steele, The Spectator, ed. by Donald Bond (London: Clarendon Press, 1965), I, 121.

16 Ibid., I, 121.

17 Ibid., I, 121.

18 Cannon, Mattheson, 127.

19 Johann Mattheson, Das neu-eröffnete Orchestre (Hamburg, 1713), 231-253.

20 Ibid., 252-253: Diß wenige von der Eigenschafft eines jeden Toni allhier den Curieusen zugefallen gemeldet worden ist, könte eine sehr große Discussion leiden, wie denn wenn alles, was davon zu sagen oder zu gedencken ist, solte angeführet werden, ein jedger Tohn wol ein eignes Capitel füllen würde; allein je mehr man sich bestreben wolte, etwas positives davon zu statuieren, je mehr contradicentes würden sich vielleicht finden, sintemahl die Meinungen in dieser Materie fast unzehlig sind, davon ich keine andere Raison, als den Unterschied der Menschlichen Complexionen zu geben weiss, als wodurch es Zweifels frey hauptsächlich geschehen mag, daß ein Tohn, der einem Sanguinischen Temperament lustig und ermunternd scheinet, einem Phlegmatischen träge, kläglich und betrübt vorkommt, u.s.w. derowegen wir uns hierbey auch nich länter aufhalten, sondern einem jeden nochmahls die Freyheit gerne lassen wollen, daß er einem oder andern Tohn solche Eigenschafften beylege, die mit seiner natürlichen Zuneigung am besten übereinkommen.

21 Alexander Malcolm, A Treatise of Music: Speculative, Practical, and Historical (Edinburgh, 1721), 455.

22 Ibid., 589.

23 Ibid., 597-599.

24 See Herbert M. Schueller, "The Use and Decorum of Music as Described in British Literature, 1700-1780," Journal of the History of Ideas, XIII (1952), 73-93.

Schueller's assumption that the concept of the affections was universally accepted in Britain seems simplistic.

25 John Wilson, Roger North on Music: Being a Selection from his Essays written during the years c.1695-1728 (London: Novello, 1959), 111.

26 Ibid., 111.

27 Ibid., 118-119.

28 Ibid., 122-123.

29 James Ralph, The Touchstone: or, Historical, Critical, Political, and Theological Essays on the reigning Diversions of the Town (London, 1728), 17.

30 Ibid., 29.

31 Johann Mattheson, Das forschende Orchestre (Hamburg, 1721), 64: Es könne das Gehör, das Gemüth und desselben Affecten am hefftigsten rege gemacht.

32 Ibid., 65-65n: ...unmittelbaren Zugang zum Geist des Menschen verstatten...

33 Johann Mattheson, Critica musica (Hamburg, 1722-1725), I, 306: ...den Affect hindern, bedecken, verwirren, verdunkeln und verkleistern...

34 Ibid., II, 331: Kein Grammaticus, kein Redner, kan so sprechen oder schreiben, als die Klänge thun können!

35 George Buelow, "Rhetoric and Music," in New Grove's Dictionary, 15, 793-803.

36 Johann David Heinichen, Der General-Baß in der Composition (Dresden, 1728), 30: Unsere Gedäncken aber auff gute Ideen zu leiten, und die natürliche Fantasie auffzumuntern, solches kan meines erachtens nicht besser geschehen, als durch die oratorischen Locos Topicos.

37 Ibid., 2n: Da wir nun einhellig gestehen müssen, daß unser finis musices sey, die Affecten zu bewegen.

38 Ernst Gottlieb Baron, Untersuchung des Instruments der Lauten (Nuremberg, 1727), 50; trans. by Douglas Alton

Smith (Redondo Beach, California: Instrumenta Antiqua, 1976), 50-51:...dass weilen diejenigen, die solches erzehlen, zu solchen Zeiten gelebet, da man mehr Fabeln als Wahrheiter gehört, die gefährlich, als man sie ausgegeben, gewesen sey.

39 Ibid., 117; 140: Ein virtuöser Musicus muss diese Qualitäten alle besitzen.

40 Ibid., 119; 142-143: Die Kunst-Regeln sind nur schwache Mittel, dadurch wir unsern verderbten Wesen in etwas zu Hülffe kommen.

41 John Christopher Pepusch, A Treatise of Harmony (London, 1731), 11.

42 Ibid., 4.

43 John Frederick Lampe, The Art of Musick (London, 1740), 5.

44 Ibid., 1.

45 Johann Adolph Scheibe, Critischer Musicus (Hamburg, 1738), 40, 108.

46 Ibid., 3, 21.

47 Ibid., Stück 67.

48 Ibid., 42, 128: So viel ist gewiss, daß je näher wir in der Musik den Regeln der Redekunst und Dichtkunst zu kommen suchen, desto gewisser werden wir auch die Vernunft und die Natur erreichen: und je mehr wir uns bemühen werden, das Schöne und das Vortreffliche einer Rede oder eines Gedichtes zu entdecken und uns nützlich zu machen, desto näher werden wir auch in der Music dem guten Geschmack kommen, der bisher den meisten Musicverständigen noch fast gänzlich unbekannt gewesen ist.

49 Immanuel Wilheim, "J. A. Scheibe: German Musical Thought in Transition" (Ph.D. dissertation, University of Illinois, 1963), 93, 103.

50 Ibid., 151-174.

51 Ibid., 28, 10: Die Figuren sind ja selbst eine Sprache der Affecten, wie solches der Herr Prof. Gottsched in seiner _Critischen Dichtkunst_ aus dem berühmten P. Lami ausführlicher erinnert.

52 Wilheim, "Scheibe," 94; Scheibe, _Critischer Musicus_, 70, 345: Seine Melodien müssen auch ohne Worte die Zuhörer bewegen und einnehmen. Und so muss er also alle Leidenschaften und Gemüthsbewegungen in seiner völligen Gewalt haben, und immer eine neue Aufmerksamkeit erwecken können.

53 Lorenz Mizler, _Die neu-eröffnete musicalische Bibliothek_ (Leipzig, 1736-1754), I, i, 5, 34n: Das ist gewiss, daß alle Dur-Thone munter scharff und lustig, hingegen alle Moll-Thone, sittsam angenehm und traurig klingen, welches die Erfahrung beweiset. Weiter muss man aber nicht gehen.

54 Ibid., I, i, v, 2, 2.

55 Ibid., II, iii, 4, 72-119.

56 Ibid., I, vi, 2, 39.

57 Ibid., II, i, 1, 1-27: Versuch eines Beweisses, daß ein Singspiel oder eine Oper nicht gut seyn könne.

58 Ibid., II, i, 1, 20.

59 Ibid., II, i, 1, 21.

60 Ibid., II, i, 1, 20n.

61 Johann Mattheson, _Der vollkommene Capellmeister_ (Hamburg, 1738), 105; trans. by Ernest C. Harriss (Ann Arbor: UMI Research Press, 1981), 256-257: die Bewegung der Gemüther und Leidenschafften der Seele von ganz was anders, nehmlich von der geschickten Einrichtung einer verständlichen, deutlichen und nachdrücklichen Melodie abhänget.

62 Ibid., 200; 413.

63 Ibid, 109; 263: Diese Anmerckung könnten sich über gantze Völckerschafften erstrecken, denen man gar wol

überhaupt und in gewissem Verstande ein allgemeines Temperament beilegen.

CHAPTER V

MUSIC AS AN IMITATION OF NATURE

Few ancient concepts about the arts influenced eighteenth-century thought more than that of imitation. This is sometimes referred to as Aristotelian mimesis (imitation) but the concept predates Aristotle, and even Plato.[1] One can see why such an attitude would find widespread approval among eighteenth-century writers. Nature was regarded as the model from which art should take her inspiration. As Alexander Pope wrote in his Essay on Criticism (1711):

> First follow Nature, and your judgement frame
> By her just standard, which is still the same:
> Unerring Nature, still divinely bright,
> One clear, unchang'd, and universal light,
> Life, force, and beauty, must to all impart,
> At once the source, and end, and test of Art.
>
> (Part I, 68-73)

Goethe felt art had to be "zugleich natürlich und rationell" and chose to support his arguments by describing the works of Leonardo da Vinci--the works he felt most strongly represented perfection.[2] Such discussions of the natural in art are, of course, manifestations of what Arthur Lovejoy termed "rationalistic primitivism", i.e., the idea common during the Enlightenment that the closer one came to nature the better one apprehended the truth.[3] The longing for simplicity can also be seen as the desire of eighteenth-century writers "to purge their minds of 'prejudices' and so to fix their attention upon the central, simple truths which they had really always known."[4] Yet another attraction for the eighteenth-century mind was the important part the concept of imitation had played in Greco-Roman artistic theory. As attractive as the concept was to eighteenth-century literary theorists, however, writers on music often found it a stumbling block. Did music imitate nature? Though some writers, like Addison, did not address the question extensively, others were preoccupied with it. Before a discussion of eighteenth-century attitudes, some preliminary comments on the ancient thoughts which inspired them are necessary.

Greek Thought on Imitation

For Plato, the theory of imitation played a crucial role in his philosophy of art.[5] This outlook was, in general, a negative one. First, because Plato viewed the world as an imperfect reproduction of an ideal, reality was automatically placed on a lower plane. Second, the arts were responsible for taking already imperfect reality and producing yet another copy of it. In Book Ten of the

Republic, for example, Socrates presents the three distinct forms of a bed (the ideal, the actual bed, and a painting of it).[6] Plato found the painter something of a Sophist, since the painter paints an untrue version of the bed to make it look better than it is. In this way he is more like a cosmetician, who reproduces the illusion of health, but has no true knowledge of it. For this reason Plato takes a grim attitude toward artists, especially poets. "If they [poets] really knew how to build ships and command troops, they would do those useful things rather than write about people doing them; if they knew the nature of a good life or a good state, they would have had some influence on citizens and governments."[7]

What was Aristotle's concept of imitation? Surprisingly enough, the adage "art imitates nature" (especially popular in the eighteenth century) cannot be supported by his views. Indeed, Aristotle considered imitation a process of some complexity, dividing it into three parts: character (moral attributes which may be seen as constant), motion (emotions which are transient and express mood), and action (in both the inward and outward sense). All three of these parts form a unit which equal an "imitation." This imitation was seen by Aristotle as a human experience--the universe of animals and landscapes was not the universe which was to be imitated by art, but instead the universe of the human soul.[8] To Plato art was merely a mirror, an imperfect rendering of the ultimate reality. To Aristotle art could improve upon nature and give it a completeness it lacked.[9] This disagreement between Plato and Aristotle had important ramifications for eighteenth-century writers, many of whom invested considerable time and effort attempting to reconcile a mistaken notion about Aristotle's theory of art's "imitation" of nature with Plato's negative attitude toward art itself. By the beginning of the eighteenth century, imitation had lost its original meaning and was regarded as a kind of natural verisimilitude.[10]

Eighteenth-Century Thought on Imitation

The concept of imitation was extremely important to eighteenth-century writers. Walter Serauky viewed the first fifty years of the century as an exposition and development of the theory of imitation, and maintained that the concept stood as a central axis for all the aesthetic views of the day.[11] James Anderson Winn's monograph on relationships between poetry and music includes a chapter devoted to the eighteenth century entitled "Imitations."[12] Certainly, one of the most important works of the eighteenth century, Charles Batteux's *Les beaux arts réduits à un même principe* (1746) manifests a preoccupation with the term. Batteux presented a system of the arts structured around his own interpretation of imitation. As Ernst Cassirer has pointed out, the title of Batteux's work betrays a rationalistic viewpoint: "Just as there are universal and unbreakable laws of nature, there must be the same types of laws, with equal dignity as well, for the imitation of nature. And finally, all of these separate laws must have one common basis, an axiom of imitation, which encompasses and orders all other laws."[13] Batteux's concept of the basic principle is nothing more than Aristotle's own theory about art as the imitator of the "possible" as presented in Nicolas Boileau-Despreaux's *L'art poétique* (1674).[14]

As far as music was concerned, the strict attitude of imitation as somehow caught up in verisimilitude led to real problems. The concept of imitation, especially in the hands of critics influenced by Boileau, was used as a means of condemning opera, and other types of music.[15] J. C. Gottsched, the major German literary figure of the early eighteenth century, wrote: "One must either leave his understanding at home and just bring his ears with him when he goes to the opera, or one must force oneself to tolerate it."[16] Opera was not alone in being condemned. In Britain, especially, instrumental music was viewed with distrust. James Brown wrote in 1763 that instrumental music was "a kind of half-life or lesser part" of the art.[17] The historian Herbert Schueller summed up the problem well:

> Poetry said something, music did not. The one was a divine science, and the other, no matter how well its name celebrated the memory of the circle of muses, ran only a poor third in the artistic race. Painting, because of its ability to portray "reality" came in second. 18

Bellamy Hosler has used the changing concepts of imitation as a means of organizing her study of instrumental music in eighteenth-century Germany. The attitude that instrumental music could not affect the listener deeply eventually was transformed when writers like Sulzer placed music in a "more appropriate category--that of the sublime."[19] The eighteenth century could be seen as the point when theories of imitation were finally dropped. They could no longer deal with the popular phenomenon of instrumental music. By the late eighteenth century Sulzer solved the problem--in his own eyes at least--by stating that of all the arts, only painting really imitated nature.[20] Early eighteenth-century writers on music sought solutions as well, though frequently more elaborate ones.

It is with the discussion of imitation that we come to an important difference between attitudes in eighteenth-century Germany and Britain. Germany had, by 1700, a vital and steadily growing tradition of writers on music. Printz and Werckmeister, Kuhnau and Kircher--all served as models for later figures, especially Johann Mattheson. In their works, written by men who were practicing musicians (with the exception of Kircher), the literary and religious outlooks of the day were tempered by their own love of the art. Thus, while there might be distrust toward music in some religious circles, German musicians were quick to defend themselves, and often used the writings of important German theologians (Luther, for example) to support their positions. Similarly, in Germany anti-musical prejudices of some literary figures, notably Gottsched, were not enough to counter-balance the growing interest in instrumental music and opera. Britain presents us with a different picture. Here there was no tradition of musical journalism, and when music was discussed the authors were rarely musicians. The religious wars which had rocked Britain during the seventeenth century had left patronage systems a shambles. This, combined with the negative attitudes toward music and musicians held by church figures, made it difficult for the depreciation of the art by literary figures to be rebutted. There were some men of letters who did appreciate music, however, and attempted to integrate it into their aesthetic outlooks. Joseph Addison, for instance, without understanding music in any profound way, described it as an art capable of expressing sublime emotion, thus anticipating Sulzer by nearly seventy years. Still, Addison's writings on music were not able to alter the views which had taken firm hold during the previous century. In Germany the failure of music to fit within systems of imitation led to new and important developments in aesthetics. In Britain the theory of imitation, and the failure of music to fit into that theory, may have contributed to a long period of musical inactivity.

Mattheson's Early Attitudes Toward Imitation

In *Das neu-eröffnete Orchestre* Mattheson uses the term *Nachahmung* (imitation) in two contexts. The first, and for our purposes less important, involves the imitation of foreign musical styles.[21] The second context is that of Aristotelian *mimesis*, an area which Mattheson discusses in some detail. He first approaches the problem while discussing the art of scenic design at the opera:

> For, whoever wishes to follow mere Nature very strictly in painting will never achieve [his aim], nor even be called a painter but only a copyist: thus, whoever wishes merely to represent simple Nature, without any embellishment, will do very badly. 22

This statement places Mattheson squarely in the tradition of Aristotle. One must imitate not what is, but what might be.

Mattheson addresses *mimesis* more thoroughly in his chapter entitled "Solution to the Question whether Music or Painting should be more highly considered." Here he presents the question of *mimesis* as it relates not to painting, but to music. In the course of his discussion Mattheson notes that music does not ornament or copy nature at all: music is nature. This observation is interesting when one considers later controversies on the subject of the "naturalness" of music, specifically that involving J. S. Bach, J. A. Scheibe, and Johann Abraham Birnbaum just two decades later. In 1737 Scheibe attacked Bach's dense polyphonic style, commenting that it was wrong to so "ornament" nature; Birnbaum responded in Bach's defense.[23] Goldschmidt and Serauky asserted that this controversy remained current until the theory of imitation was shaken by the observation of Caspar Ruetz in 1754, a Capellmeister in Lübeck, that music was not a copy of nature, but nature itself.[24] Yet Mattheson had made the same point forty-one years before! It also seems probable that Ruetz himself got his ideas from Mattheson. The two were friends and Mattheson wrote a lament on the death of Ruetz in 1755.[25]

Once one begins to see how many different attitudes toward imitation existed, side-by-side, even among German writers, the evolutionary discussions of Serauky, Goldschmidt, and even some modern historians, seem less valid. Certainly, Mattheson is due some credit for his presentation of mimesis in Das neu-eröffnete Orchestre. In his comparison of music and painting he set an important precedent for German writers on music.

Imitation in the 1720s

Although imitation was not an important issue for Malcolm, nor most British writers, he did touch on it. Perhaps Malcolm presents his concept of the relation between music and nature best when he says:

> As to the Invention [i.e., of music], I think there is enough said already to show that Musick is natural to Mankind; and therefore instead of Inventors, the Enquiry ought properly to be about the Improvers of it. 26

Music was, then, a natural product of man. It is in this light that Malcolm's reiteration of Pythagorean concepts must be seen:

> But Pythagoras said he perceived and understood the Celestial Harmony by a peculiar Favour of that Spirit to whom he owed his Life, as Jamblichus reports of him, who says, that tho' he never sang or played an Instrument himself, yet by an inconceivable Sort of Divinity, he taught others to imitate the Celestial Musick of the Spheres, by Instruments and Voice: For according to him, all the Harmony of sounds here below, is but an Imitation, and that imperfect too, of the other. 27

Malcolm avoids the problem connected with questions of Aristotelian _mimesis_ by ignoring the issue. Perhaps he was unfamiliar with the controversies raging in France. More likely, he did not find the issue relevant to his discussions, since, like Mattheson, Malcolm felt music was obviously a part of nature itself. Malcolm's most interesting comments about imitation and music occur in his discussion of the merits of ancient and modern artists. One of the primary improvements of modern artists, according to Malcolm, was that they no longer simply imitate the obvious aspects of nature--that is, the passions themselves--but go beyond that into the world of the understanding. "We have," he notes, "also a new Art, whose End is rather to entertain the Understanding, than to move particular Passions."[28] This, as we shall see, is an important part of Malcolm's concept of the imagination.

Music, according to Roger North, is an imitative art, a "pantomime" of all the actions of man. The duty of the listener is to recreate in his own mind whatever state the composer represents in his music.[29] North also points out that music imitates nature in a general way only: to imitate words too specifically, we are told, can be ridiculous. A composer who misunderstands the statement "they laugh at my dolorous complaints" might present joyous music as an accompaniment to the words, etc.[30] In his discussion of instrumental music North notes that the composer sometimes must decide what passion is to be presented without the help of a text to guide him. Though weddings and "triumphs" provide little problem, since the affections are obvious enough, other moods are more difficult to capture. No matter what passion is to be set, however, the composer must present those affections most beneficial to humanity since the audience will act in conformity with it.[31] It is at this point that North discusses the similar duties of the painter, poet, and composer, using the example of Raphael's painting mentioned above.

North also makes direct reference to music's ability to imitate various emotional states in his presentation of the art of playing organ voluntaries:

> A voluntere thus quallifyed may take his seat...and there he may put in execution all the various states of body and mind, by a musicall imitation, (as I have suggested) that his humour or capriccio, as well as good understanding and sence, shall in his fancy conjure up. He will be grave, reasonable, merry, capering and dancing, artificiall, Malencholly, querolous, stately and proud, or submissive and humble, buisie, in haste, frighted, quarrell and fight, run, walk, or consider, search, rejoyce, prattle, weep, laugh insult, triumph; and at last, perhaps, vanish out

> os sight all at once; or end in very good temper, and as one layd downe to rest or sleep. 32

For North even instrumental music was capable of imitating many of man's emotions. In this respect North was no conservative: music, even instrumental music, was imitative since it imitated the passions, natural to all humanity.

The question whether music could be labeled a mimetic art is dealt with by James Ralph in a manner similar to Malcolm's: he avoids it. First of all, Ralph chose only to discuss operatic music, and regarded instrumental music as incapable of moral effect.[33] There is no discussion in the Touchstone of instrumental music. In his discussion of opera Ralph shows disapproval of the powerful influence of foreign artists, especially the Italians. Ralph, however, supports the idea of opera, and addresses each of these objections: 1) that the language cannot be understood, since it is foreign; 2) that the airs are beautiful, but recitative should not be allowed; 3) that foreign performers are paid too much; and 4) that the opera willfully violates all acknowledged poetic laws.[34] Ralph refutes all of them but the response to the last is the most interesting. There are those, Ralph says, who insist that matters of artistic judgement require strict rules. These people, who (we are told) are themselves incapable of creating anything, damn all works which defy their standards and attempt to judge opera using the rules of Aristotle and Rene Rapin. These attempts are doomed, however, because opera transcends such regulation and "despises the Power or Limitations of a Parliment of Criticks."[35] Ralph found questions about the mimetic qualities of music superfluous. If opera is "subject to no poetical laws" it would seem logical to assume that music, in general, was an art which had no need to conform to literary conventions. In a sense, Ralph and Malcolm presaged writers of the next generation who found discussions of imitation in music irrelevant.

Mattheson upholds the superiority of music over the other arts in Das forschende Orchestre, calling painting and sculpture, for example, mere "apes of nature," and noting that, without rhythm, poetry "may not exist." Only music can raise the passions "without the slightest imitation of external things."[36] Mattheson turns the argument of literary critics around by insisting that music, because it does not imitate nature, is the superior, not the inferior, art. He continues his depreciation of the other arts in a poem:

> So may painting please only the eyes;
> Take them, poetry, both eyes and ears:
> Music should be, however, prized above both:
> It must be for eye and heart, for ear and soul.
> Here can neither the deaf or blind judge,
> because for them its all the same--tone, picture, poetry,
> What are colors? Dust. The best words? Wind.
> Only beautiful melody lasts forever. 37

Mattheson rejects the arguments of Bokemeyer, the defender of canon and fugue, with the argument that his art is (when taken to extremes) "unnatural". The following "conversation" has been created out of Bokemeyer's comments and Mattheson's footnotes to them in Critica Musica:

> Bokemeyer: If an artist wishes to bring forth something excellent, he must properly combine nature and art.
> Mattheson: I say, Nature must make the beginning: else the art cannot be brought forth. It cannot be called combination:for the word implies a certain parity.

> _Bokemeyer_: Nature and art are dissimilar like _majus et minus_, like master and servant, or woman and maid, or _dux_ and _comes_.
> _Mattheson_: _Dux_ and _comes_, _majus et minus_, are not like master and servant, woman and maid. Whoever can write fugues knows well, that _dux_ is merely _primus inter pares_.
> _Bokemeyer_: For art is only an ape of nature.
> _Mattheson_: True. How can one then combine them?
> _Bokemeyer_: The artist must imitate nature, and _imitatio Naturae_ is the goal of all arts.
> _Mattheson_: Such statements would be contradicted by no one. How does this serve the artificial _canonibus_, however?
> _Bokemeyer_: The more similar a work of art is to nature, the more perfect it is.
> _Mattheson_: I would gladly have believed this, if the previous statement had not appeared. For it seems quite certain to me, that an ape is worth several dollars more, when he comes close to humans with his gestures. But, that is merely a poor perfection, which indeed brings forth laughter, amazement, and a pastime; but has no further use. 38

The artificial art of canon does not have any relation to nature, according to Mattheson, who supports his argument for melody by using imitation of nature as a central argument. The apparently contrary lines of the argument--that music does not imitate nature, and that canon is undesirable since it does not imitate nature--can only be reconciled if one is willing to accept Mattheson's statements in the previous decade that music was itself a part of nature. Mattheson never saw the contradiction in his arguments, and such contradictions are frequent in his writings. To Mattheson music and its imitation meant different things at different times.

Imitation in the 1730s

Although John Frederick Lampe was no stranger to the debate on imitation and music, he avoided discussing categories of imitation and focused instead on the importance of sense experience. "Art refines and embellishes the materials which Nature produces," Lampe said, pointing out that "art must keep as close to Nature as possible."[39] Art is never so perfect, Lampe maintains, "as when it imitates Nature most."[40] Even so, Lampe was really more interested in nature itself, not in a concept of imitation.

The concept of naturalness and its relationship with the currents in musical style during the 1730s dominated J. A. Scheibe's thought. This is clearly seen in his dispute over Bach. Scheibe also attempted to discover "the natural" in specific types of musical composition, particularly the recitative--a search which led him to the works of Addison. These three issues, nature, the Bach controversy, and recitative, provide the basis for our examination of Scheibe's attitude toward imitation.

To Scheibe, nature was the handmaiden of God, and her works were great and wonderful.[41] Man's drive for music was, according to Scheibe, nothing less than the divine element contained in nature. To explain man's musicality as the mere imitation of birds, a practice even Gottsched joked about, was to deny this divine element.[42] As one might expect, Scheibe was not interested in yet another reworking of eighteenth-century literary doctrine. Instead, he followed Mattheson in maintaining that music was as much a part of nature as the beings which produce it. In the following excerpt Scheibe summarizes his view of imitation in music:

> That music deals with the imitation of nature; that its beauties are based upon and advanced by good taste; that it must attain its goals by moving the spirits [passions]; that is must further express itself in a particular style and that this style must agree in all parts with the style of poetry and eloquence and that it finally is never so near to attaining greatness and fortunate expression as now, since the liberal arts have reached a completely different and rational reputation, so may one now tell me if all of this improvement in music is related to the improvement in poetry and rhetoric, and if these may be improved even more. 43

Scheibe naturally answered this question in the positive, and pointed out the important roles played by imitation, taste, and concept of the affections.

Scheibe's emphasis on the natural in music is nowhere more evident than in his criticism of Bach.[44] His comments reflected his attitude that art must be natural, an attitude which carried with it the aesthetic of the highly decorated melodic style of Scheibe's favorite composer, Telemann. Buelow points out that Scheibe's attack was actually the articulation of the new style in music then taking hold in Germany.[45] Bach's music, in Scheibe's estimation, did not place the proper emphasis on melody. In his devotion to melody Scheibe was preceded by Heinichen and Mattheson, but he was the first effective spokesman for the new style in his generation. His criticism of Bach is an outcry against music which was difficult for the listener to comprehend, but also a plea for simplicity and a "return to nature" in music.

One of Scheibe's major preoccupations was the recitative, a subject which comes up frequently in

Critischer Musicus, devoting an entire essay to the subject in the second edition of the work.[46] Both G. J. Skapski and Gregory Calmus have mentioned Scheibe's interest in the works of Addison.[47] It is in the essay on recitative that Scheibe revealed his familiarity with the Briton, and included Spectator No. 29 (translated by none other than Louise Adelgunde Gottsched, the wife of the literary critic).[48] Scheibe's interest in Spectator No. 29 is understandable. This number expressed many of Addison's views on music, notably that the recitative of each nation should reflect the qualities of the native tongue. This was in keeping with Scheibe's own concept of the natural in music, specifically that recitative--as a part of music--should not be banned from sacred music.[49]

Scheibe's references to Addison in this essay, and in other sections of Critischer Musicus illustrate the influence of British writers on German musical thought. Also of significance is the vehicle which made Scheibe's awareness of Addison possible--a translation of the Spectator done by Frau Gottsched. Her and her husband's admiration for Addison is testimony to the necessity for a re-evaluation of the view that Gottsched was merely a representative for French literary theory.[50]

Lorenz Mizler had a firm belief in the concept of imitation. "It is an undeniable truth," he wrote, "[that] all arts originate in an imitation of nature."[51] As with the affections, Mizler made his position clear by disagreeing with a contemporary, in this case Scheibe:

> In the eighth number [of Scheibe's Critischer Musicus] one reads: Art must, in general, assure that nature is allowed to bring its strengths to the light of day. This is actually a false thought. What is art? An imitation of nature. If then art, which imitates

> nature, brings forth something orderly and rational, then the orderliness and rationality must have existed previously--or else they could not have arisen from an imitation. 52

Though both men agreed that art imitated nature, the process of imitation was a matter of debate. Mizler's own conception of imitation is best revealed in a comment made in his Musikalischer Staarstecher: "Music is actually nothing less than a Geometry of tones."[53] Mizler defended the concept of imitation by blending the philosophies of Wolff and Leibniz and finding in nature a kind of mathematical universe and relating it to music. Whether he did this out of a desire to create a real system of knowledge about music, or to create a "science" acceptable enough to intellectual circles in Leipzig to assure himself a professorship there is a question which may never be answered.[54]

Mizler relies on his conception of the natural in music to refute the arguments against opera--specifically recitative--found in Gottsched's essay on opera (itself an imitation of Addison's Spectator No. 29). Gottsched criticized recitative, pointing out that performers no longer sang in a manner compatible with their native tongue, their throats, or the passion intended.[55] This criticism, and Gottsched's observation that singing a conversation was inherently unnatural, are considered unfair by Mizler. First, a competent composer would write music appropriate for the language, performer's ability, and the given passion. Second, it had been a practice since ancient times to sing words originally intended to be spoken, hence it could not be unnatural.[56] Going one step further, Mizler maintained that unrhymed poetry in recitative was perhaps more natural than rhymed. Commenting on Ludwig's essay he noted:

> What is more natural: if I attempt to make what is already in nature clearer, I mean, if I make my speech orderly and recitative-like in song, or if I speak in rhymed verses? 57

When one recalls the controversies in Germany surrounding the unrhymed poetry of Milton, for example, this remark is striking. Mizler was perfectly willing to go against his teacher, Gottsched, in his defense of opera--a willingness which shows how discussions about music by literary theorists were simply no longer adequate.

Although imitation, as it related to "naturalness" in music, had been one of Johann Mattheson's preoccupations in the 1720s, even more interest in the concept is revealed in Capellmeister. This is best seen in his remark that composers who write "full-voiced, artificial counterpoint" do so to hide their inability at writing good melodies.[58] Mattheson called these composers of Augenmusik swine, though he never attacked specific composers openly as Scheibe did.

In the third section of Mattheson's Capellmeister he addressed the topic of imitation in detail, providing three meanings of the term:

> Now imitation means three things in music. For first we find opportunity to practice such with all sorts of natural things and affections, wherein the very greatest source for invention is to be found, as has been said in its place. Second, there is that effort which one makes to imitate this or that master's and Musician's work which is quite a good thing so long as no actual musical thievery is accomplished in the process. Third, imitation is that pleasant competition which various voices practice with all freedom among

> one another on certain formulas, passages or short phrases. 59

One other type of imitation is mentioned by Mattheson, however, this being the imitation, during a recitative, of the various sounds of things being discussed--i.e., thunder, turbulence, confusion, etc.[60] Mattheson ascribes this type of imitation to the French, and attacks the practice severely.

It is regrettable that Mattheson did not provide any more information about the first type of imitation mentioned in his list. This points to another change in Mattheson's views in the 1730s, namely a decrease of his interest in the philosophical aspects of "naturalness" coupled with a decrease in the frequency of references to Wolff and Locke, men he had discussed extensively in previous decades. Of primary importance is the fact that Mattheson continued to defend his statements made twenty-five years earlier, that music was a part of nature, not an imitation of it. By the 1730s his dissatisfaction with a narrow definition of the concept of imitation in music was shared by most of his contemporaries.

1 Anna Tumarkin, "Die Überwindung der Mimesislehre in der Kunsttheorie des XVIII. Jahrhunderts," in *Festgabe Samuel Singer* (Tübingen: J. C. B. Mohr, 1930), 40.

2 Ibid., 40.

3 Arthur O. Lovejoy, "The Parallel of Deism and Classicism," in *Essays in the History of Ideas* (Baltimore: Johns Hopkins Press, 1948), 78-98.

4 Ibid., 84.

5 See Monroe Beardsley, *Aesthetics from Classical Greece to the Present* (New York: Macmillan, 1966), 33-39.

6 J. G. Warry, *Greek Aesthetic Theory* (London: Oxford University Press, 1962), 62-63.

7 Beardsley, *Aesthetics*, 38. Plato's discussion can be found in *Republic*, 598-601.

8 Butcher, *Aristotle*, 124.

9 Ibid., 158.

10 Jean H. Hagstum, *The Sister Arts* (Chicago: University of Chicago Press, 1958), 83.

11 Serauky, *Nachahmung*, 3.

12 James Anderson Winn, *Unsuspected Eloquence: A History of the Relations between Poetry and Music* (New Haven: Yale University Press, 1981), 194ff.

13 Ernst Cassirer, *Die Philosophie der Aufklärung* (Tübingen, 1973), 375.

14 Tumarkin, "Überwindung," 43.

15 Wilhelm Bernhard Schwann, "Die opernästhetischen Theorien der deutschen klassischen Dichter" (Ph.D. dissertation, University of Bonn, 1928), 6.

16 Johann Christian Gottsched, *Der Biedermann* in *Gesammelte Schriften* (Berlin: Gottsched Verlag, 1903), III, 219.

17 See J. Draper, Eighteenth-Century English Aesthetics: A Bibliography (Heidelberg, 1931), 81.

18 Herbert Schueller, "Literature and Music as Sister Arts: An Aspect of Aesthetic Theory in Eighteenth-Century Britain," Philological Quarterly, XXVI (1947), 195.

19 Bellamy Hosler, Changing Aesthetic Views of Instrumental Music in 18th-Century Germany (Ann Arbor: UMI Research Press, 1981), 143.

20 See Johann Georg Sulzer, Allgemeine Theorie der schönen Künste (Facs. ed; Hildesheim: Georg Olms, 1969), III, 278.

21 Johann Mattheson, Das neu-eröffnete Orchestre (Hamburg, 1713), 218.

22 Ibid., 166-167: Denn wer in der Mahlerei der blossen Natur gar zu genau folgen will, der wird nimmer resultieren, ja nicht einmahl eines Mahlers, sondern nur eines Copiisten Nahmen verdienen: also, wer scenicis nichts vorstellen wolte, als die simple Natur, ohne einigen Zierath, der würde blutschlecht ankommen, und wenige Surprisen machen.

23 See George Buelow. "In Defence of J. A. Scheibe against J. S. Bach," in Procedings of the Royal Music Association CI (1974-1975), 85; H. Keller, "Johann Adolph Scheibe und Johann Sebastian Bach," in Musik und Verlag: Karl Vötterle zum 65. Geburtstag (Kassel: Bärenreiter, 1968), 383.

24 Walter Serauky, Die musikalsiche Nachahmungsästhetik im Zeitraum von 1700 bis 1850 (Münster: Helios Verlag, 1929), 77.

25 George Buelow, "Ruetz," in New Grove's Dictionary, 16, 317-318.

26 Alexander Malcolm, A Treatise of Music: Speculative, Practical, and Historicale (Edinburgh, 1721), 464.

27 Ibid., 454.

28 Ibid., 600-601.

29 John Wilson, Roger North on Music: Being a Selection from his Essays written during the years c.1695-1728 (London: Novello, 1959), 110.

30 Ibid., 112-113.

31 Ibid., 115.

32 Ibid., 139-140.

33 James Ralph, The Touchstone: or, Historical, Critical, Political, and Theological Essays on the reigning Diversions of the Town (London, 1728), 3.

34 Ibid., 12-13.

35 Ibid., 19.

36 Johann Mattheson, Das forschende Orchestre (Hamburg, 1721), xii.

37 Johann Mattheson, Critica musica (Hamburg, 1722-1725), I, 95:
So mag das Mahler-Werk die Augen nur ergetzen;
Nimm denn, du Dichterey, so Aug' als Ohren ein:
Die Tonkunst soll man doch noch über beyde schätzen:
Sie muss für Aug' und Herz, für Ohr und Seele seyn.
Hier gibt den Ausschlag nicht der Taube, noch der Blinde,
Als denen einerley, Ton, Bild und Poesie,
Was sind Farben? Staub. Die besten Worte? Winde.
Nur bleibt in Ewigkeit die schöne Melodie.

38 Ibid., I, 330-332. Bokemeyer's statements appear in the text, Mattheson's responses in the footnotes. Some steps in the argument have been ommitted for the sake of brevity.
Bokemeyer: Wofern ein Künstler was fürtreffliches herfürbringen soll, so muss er Natur und Kunst gehörig combiniren.
Mattheson: Ich sage, das Naturell muss den Anfang machen: sonst ist die Kunst nicht aus der Stelle zu bringen. Combiniren kann man es auch gar nicht heißen: denn das Wort erfordert eine gewisse paritatem...

Bokemeyer: Nature und Kunst sind unterschieden ut majus et minus, wie Herr und Knecht, oder Frau und Magd, ut dux et comes.
Mattheson: Dux et comes, majus et minus sind nicht wie Herr und Knecht, wie Frau und Magd. Wer Fugen machen kann, weiß wohl, daß Dux nur primus inter pares sey.
Bokemeyer: Denn die Kunst ist nur ein Affe der Natur.
Mattheson: Wahr! Wie kann man sie denn combiniren?
Bokemeyer: In diesem Falle muss der Künstler die Natur imitiren, und imitatio Naturae ist der Zweck in allen Künsten.
Mattheson: Solchen Sätzen wird kein Mensch widersprechen. Was ist aber den künstlichen canonibus damit gedienet?
Bokemeyer: Je ähnlicher nun ein Kunst-Werk der Natur ist, desto vollkommener ist es.
Mattheson: Das hatte ich gerne glauben wollen, wenn gleich die vorhergehenden so genannt General-Sätze gar nicht erschienen wären. Denn es stehet ganz gewiss bey mir fest, daß ein Affe alsdenn etliche Thaler mehr werth sey, wenn er mit seinen gestibus dem Menschen sehr nähe kömmt. Aber, das ist doch eine schlechte Vollkommenheit, die zwar ein Gelächter, eine Verwunderung und einen Zeitvertreib zu Wege bringt; doch weiter keinen Nutzen hat.

39 John Frederick Lampe, The Art of Musick (London, 1740), 7, 20.

40 Ibid., 20.

41 Johann Adolph Scheibe, Critischer Musicus (Hamburg, 1738), 5, 36.

42 Ibid., 5, 36.

43 Ibid., 71, 357: Da die Music mit der Nachahmung der Natur zu thun hat; da sie ihre Schönheiten auf den guten Geschmack gründet und durch denselben befördert; da sie bey der Erreichung ihrer Absichten die Gemüther bewegen und einnehmen muss; da sie ferner, sich auszudrücken, einer gewissen Schreibart nötig hat, diese Schreibart aber in allen Stücken mit der Schreibart in der Poesie und Beredsamkeit übereinkommt; und da sie endlich noch niemals zu der Grösse und glücklichen Ausübung gelanget ist, als jetzo, da die vernünftigeres Ansehen gewonnen haben: So mag man mir nunmehro sagen, ob nicht auch die Verbesserung der Music an der Verbesserung der Dichtkunst und Redekunst

gelegen hat, und ob aus diesen jene nicht noch trefflicher und vollkommener verbessert werden kann?

44 Immanuel Wilheim, "J. A. Scheibe: German Musical Thought in Transition" (Ph. D. dissertation, University of Illinois, 1963), 99-106.

45 George Buelow, "Scheibe," in New Grove's Dictionary, 16, 600.

46 Scheibe, Critischer Musicus, (2nd. ed.; Hamburg, 1745), 750-795.

47 Ibid., 733-750.

48 Ibid., 737-738.

49 Ibid., 734.

50 Frau Gottsched also published a version of Addison's comedy, The Drummer (London, 1716). In his Handlexikon oder Kurzgefasstes Wörterbuch der schönen Wissenschaften und freyen Künste (Leipzig, 1760) J. C. Gottsched called Addison "one of the ablest pens of his time and his people" (eine der geschicktesten Federn seiner Zeit und seines Volkes).

51 Lorenz Mizler, Die neu-eröffnete musikalische Bibliothek (Leipzig, 1736-1754), I, v, 2, 55: Es ist eine unumstössliche Wahrheit: alle Künste bestehen in einer Nachahmung der Natur.

52 Ibid., I, v, 4, 72-73: Im achten Stück heisset es: Die Kunst muss insgemein verschaffen, daß die Natur ihre Kräfte ordentlich und vernünftig den Tag bringen kan. Es ist in Wahrheit eine falsche Gedanke. Was ist die Kunst? eine Nachahmung der Natur. Wenn also die Kunst, in dem sie der Natur nachahmet, was ordentliches und vernünftiges hervorbringet, so muß das ordentliche und vernüftige schon vorher da gewesen seyn, sonst hätte aus der Nachahmung solches nicht entstehen können.

53 Lorenz Christoph Mizler, Musikalischer Staarstecher (Leipzig, 1739-1740), 48: Nun aber ist die Musik in der That nichts anders, als eine auf die Töne gerichtete Geometrie.

54 See Franz Wöhlke, Lorenz Christoph Mizler (Würzburg: Konrad Triltsch, 1940), 8-9, 19, 95; Wilheim, "Scheibe," 70-78.

55 Mizler, Bibliothek, II, iii, 1, 14.

56 Ibid., II, iii, 1, 14n.

57 Ibid., II, i, 1, 14n: Es ist noch eine Streitige Frage, welches natürlicher ist: wenn ich meinen Vortrag gereimt, oder recitativisch singend mache?

58 Johann Mattheson, Der vollkommene Capellmeister (Hamburg, 1738), 105; trans. by Ernest C. Harriss (Ann Arbor: UMI Research Press, 1981), 256: vollstimmige Sachen, auf künstliche Contrapuncte.

59 Ibid., 331; 637: Diese Nachahmung nun hat in der Music dreierley zu bedeuten. Denn erstlich finden wir Gelegenheit, dergleichen Übung mit allerhand natürlichen Dingen und Gemüths-Neigungen anzustellen, worin schier das grösseste Hülfsmittel der Erfindung bestehet, wie an seinem Orte gesaget worden ist. Fürs andre wird diejenige Bemühung verstanden, so man sich gibt, dieses oder jenen Meisters und Ton-Künstlers Arbeit nachzumachen: welches eine gantz gute Sache ist, so lange kein förmlicher Musicalischer Raub dabey mit unterläufft. Drittens bemercket man durch die Nachahmung denjenigen angenehmen Wettstreit, welchen verschiedene Stimmen über gewisse Förmelgen, Gänge oder kurtze Sätze mit aller Freiheit unter einander führen.

60 Ibid., 334; 641.

CHAPTER VI

MUSICAL TASTE, AND TASTES

The works of writers on music in eighteenth-century Britain and Germany reflect a great interest in the concept of taste. Though the term appeared less and less frequently after the first decades of the century in musical writings, discussions of taste did mirror the eighteenth-century psyche. Ernest Tuveson, in his essay on Shaftesbury's' Characteristics, called taste the key word not only of Shaftesbury's work, but the entire age.[1] Thomas B. Gilmore, editor of a collection of eighteenth-century British writings on taste, points out that the term was so universal that writers "saw little point in lengthy analyses of it or arguments to establish reality."[2] In Germany the term occupied the attention of the foremost writers and philosophers throughout the century, whether or not one agrees with Alexander von Bormann, who sees a larger sociological phenomenon in shifts in attitudes toward taste.[3] As Lewis White Beck has pointed out, developing a theory of taste was one of the deep needs of eighteenth-century German philosophy: "the history of its taste reflects the history of German taste itself, from a philistine moralism and neoclassical imitativeness to the excesses of the Sturm und Drang."[4]

The frequent use of the term in eighteenth-century Europe was in part a manifestation of the concept of taste as a universal standard of judgement. This view, popular in the first twenty-five years of the century and presented by Shaftesbury himself, had some built-in problems. Monroe Beardsley characterized Shaftesbury's argument as a presentation of "universal standards of judgement" as based "upon fairly conventional rationalistic principles."[5] Even so, the concept was tempting, especially in an age when universality was the goal of many intellectuals. Within the ambiguity of the term writers could find those traits which suited them and a "universality" which was hardly universal.

Modern historians of taste credit Baltasar Gracian (1601-1658), a Spanish Jesuit, with making the term popular. Taste is discussed in some detail in his El Oràculo Manual y Arte de Prudentia (1647).[6] This work, translated into French in 1684 and into English one year later, was extremely popular. The early connection between taste and the court circles of Louis XIV helped this popularity. The French aristocracy found the idea that it was possible to make spontaneous judgements on art most appealing since it fit into a scheme of life which was preoccupied with the search for happiness. This happiness was achieved through art, social activities, even through imagination. Because art played such an important role in this scheme, the concept of good taste was incorporated into the aristocratic vocabulary.[7]

The concept was also popular with French writers such as Charles de Margutel de Saint-Denis Saint-Evremond (1610-1704), who opposed the excessive formalism of the *Académie Française*.[8] This institution, founded in 1635, attempted to regulate art with numerous guidelines and was supported by writers like Boileau and Rapin. For a writer like Saint-Evremond, taste was an attractive term since it allowed for an intuitive approach to art which the *Académie* did not recognize.

Taste in Britain

Discussions of taste in early eighteenth-century Britain offer some interesting variations to continental themes. Literary men defined taste by writing about what it was not. Satire was the favored vehicle, as in this anonymous poem from 1733 which describes the "woman of taste":

> Buy, that the gaping mob may stop and gaze,
> Books for their binding--pictures for their blaze;
> Holdben's and Wootton's, if they look but gay;
> And keep a spinnet, though you never play. 9

The main point of such satirical verse was, in Thomas Gilmore's words, "to call attention to those who flouted it [taste], who substituted temporary fashion or local custom for its universality."[10]

The satirical writers were joined by a number of aristocrats, often referred to as "virtuosi," who prided themselves on their education and, of course, taste. These dilettants, to whom the fields of science and history were of special interest, found the term irresistable. J. E. Spingarn remarked that the virtuosi saw "in the then more or less novel concept of 'taste' a guide-post to what they sought and a touchstone of their success in finding it."[11] The ambiguity of the term also made it more popular. Taste could mean many things, as the anonymous author of Taste and Beauty pointed out in 1732:

> Taste is a Mark so small, no common Sight
> Can guide th'uncertain Arrow to the White;
> Like Wit, and Human Humour, 'tis a Cob-web Theme,
> An unknown Substance, but familiar Name;
> All talk as if the Standard were their own,
> And each enjoy'd the sacred Text alone;
> But none essay the Bullion in the Mine,
> Or slew the Royal Impress on their Coin; 12

The same author offered his own definition of taste as well:

> Taste tc the Mind is like the Mode in Dress
> What all admire, and covet to possess;
> But oft deceiv'd in both, the publick Voice
> Mocks its own Fondness by an Idiot Choice;
> In vain light fancy roams a random Guide;
> Opinion alter, Fancy know no Bound;
> Error begins, and Folly ends the Round:
> The Want of Beauty Want of Taste betrays,
> and Elegance alone can merit Praise.
> True Taste's the Relish which the Mind receives
> From Harmony, the Joy which Beauty gives!
> 'Tis born of Genius, but 'tis nurs'd by Art,
> The Head's the Fountain, tho' it reach the Heart;
> If forms the Image in the Mind,
> 'Tis Taste Corrects what Genius has design'd:
> Nature's the Body, Genius the Soul,
> But Taste unites them both and reconciles the whole:
> As from the Stars, that gem the Brow of Night,
> Descends one common Stream of blended Light,
> So Taste must flow from Wisdom's Rays divine,
> And in one gen'ral Constellation shine. 13

Both these excerpts reveal the qualities of taste most popular in the early eighteenth century. Taste was seen as a reconciling force between Genius and Nature.

One final point should be made about the concept of taste in Britain. While French ideas about literature were always important in Britain, there was no unanimity of opinion about the value of them. In the following excerpt from John Dryden's Dedication to the Examen Poeticum one can already sense the growing self-confidence of the native English writer.

> Our authors as far surpass them (French dramatic writers) in genius as our soldiers excel theirs in courage. 'Tis true, in conduct they surpass us either way; yet that proceeds not so much from their greater knowledge, as from the difference of tastes in the two nations. They content themselves with a thin design, without episodes, and managed by a few persons. Our audience will not be pleased, but with variety of accidents, and many actors. They follow the ancients too serviley in mechanic rules, and we assume too much licence to ourselves, in keeping them only in view at too great a distance. 14

If Dryden--considered a French-oriented writer--felt that British and French tastes were so different, then one must suspect that musical tastes and attitudes differed as well.

Taste in Germany

Attitudes toward taste in Germany were affected by factors different from those in Britain. Literary men, like Gottsched, took ideas freely from various sources (especially France) and created their own unique synthesis. Religious attitudes were still strong in Germany and a social transformation of the first magnitude was occurring.

To Germans (such as A. G. Baumgarten) taste contained a clearly democratic element.[15] Taste was seen as a universal and, like reason, was considered a "given" in the equation of eighteenth-century aesthetics. A current and popular concept in intellectual circles, taste was scrutinized and analyzed in Germany on a scale unprecedented in Britain or France.

The democratic element in German attitudes toward taste was presented in the works of J. J. Bodmer and J. J. Breitinger, two Swiss whose _Discourse der Mahlern_ was modeled after Addison's _Spectator_.[16] In 1736 Bodmer's _Briefwechsel über den poetischen Geschmack_ presented the view that good taste was an inborn trait.[17] This attitude was rejected by Gottsched and other writers, including musicians. The experience of practicing musicians may have made an inborn taste seem implausible, as these remarks by J. J. Quantz show:

> Now since music is the sort of art which must be judged, not according to our own fancy, but like the other arts, according to good taste, acquired through certain rules and refined by much experience and exercises; since he who wishes to judge another ought to understand at least as much as the other, if not more; since these qualities are seldom met with in those who occupy themselves with the judging of music; since, on the contrary, the greater part of these are governed by ignorance, prejudice, and passions which hinder correct judgment; many a one would do much better if he would keep his judgment to himself and listen with greater attention, if, without judging, he can still take pleasure in music. 18

It seems understandable that writers on music agreed with the concept of an "educated taste" espoused by Gottsched, who felt taste was "the power of deciding whether a work of art was good or not (...) the word of understanding, of applying rules to ideas which the common man experiences only as emotion or spectacle."[19] Unlike literary figures like Bodmer, musicians had frequent and direct contact with their audience--experiences which were not always positive. Similarly, musicians spent much time defending their art from the accusation that it was a mere entertainment. The "taste through experience" attitude was more attractive to most musicians.

National Traits and Discussions of Taste

The most dramatic differences in national taste were probably those between the French and British. These differences may have been part of the widespread anti-French sentiment which characterized British foreign policy throughout much of the century. The competition between the countries for world domination, as well as their religious differences, made acceptance of French standards of taste impossible in Britain. These differences were mirrored in the kind of men in each nation who wrote about taste: aristocratic amateurs in France, philosophers like David Hume and Edward Burke in Britain.[20]

It was in Germany, however, that the concept underwent the most profound intellectualization. German writers examined the concept of taste with the same rigor as they had the affections, and along with the British developed their discussions of taste into aesthetic systems. Rémy Saisselin summs up the trends in the three countries by saying "the Germans intellectualized beauty; the English materialized it; the French drew distinctions."[21] While such categorizations of national thought may be dangerous, Saisselin's statements are supported by an examination of eighteenth-century sources. Discussions about differences in national tastes were extremely important in writings on music in the early eighteenth century.

Addison and Mattheson in the First Two Decades of the Eighteenth Century

The second section of Addison's Spectator No. 29 examines music--and the other arts--in a more general manner, pointing out that national preferences are revealed by the fact that what may seem "Harmony to one Ear, may be Dissonance to an- other."[22] Addison then points to the example of Lully (whose popularity the writer had witnessed first-hand during his visit to Paris in 1699) as a model of how a composer should adapt to the tastes of a different culture:

> Signior Baptist Lully...did not pretend to extirpate the French Musick, and plant the Italian in its stead; but only to Cultivate and Civilize it with innumerable Graces and Modulation which he borrow'd from the Italian. 23

It seems possible that Addison spoke here with his own bitter experience with Rosamund in mind. Thomas Clayton, after all, was hardly the "English Lully" for whom one supposes Addison had hoped.

The final paragraph of No. 29 contains some of Addison's most interesting ideas on music and the sister arts:

> I shall add no more to what I have here offer'd than that Musick, Architecture and Painting, as well as Poetry and Oratory, are to deduce their Laws and Rules from the general Sense and Taste of Mankind and not from the Principles of those Arts themselves; or in other Words, the Taste is not to conform to the Art but the Art to the Taste. Musick is not design'd to please only Chromatick Ears, but all that are capable of distinguishing harsh from disagreeable Notes. A Man of an ordinary Ear is a Judge whether a Passion is express'd in proper Sounds, and whether the Melody of those Sounds be more or less pleasing. 24

For Addison, the average listener is more properly the judge of musical excellence than specialists in the field (i.e., those of "Chromatick Ears"). One also gets the impression that "the general Sense and Taste of Mankind" points to a quality possessed innately in each individual and not developed by education or experience. This concept is in direct conflict with Addison's earlier observation, namely that tastes vary from country to country. The existence, side-by-side, of opposing concepts was not unusual in Addison's works, or those of his contemporaries.

In <u>Spectator</u> No. 29 Addison also presents his own attempt at a system by which one might unite the arts. Addison felt that the "general Sense and Taste of Mankind" could serve as a universal standard. The rules of the arts themselves should not be codified by practitioners of the arts, but by those who were to be moved by them. No matter what problems such a concept may carry with it, an attempt to find unity among the arts is an important step in the development of aesthetic thought. Addison's unifying theory was of a more original nature than that of Charles Batteux, whose ideas came thirty years later and merely reiterated ancient Greek traditions.

In the third section of Das neu-eröffnete Orchestre (Pars Tertia Judicatoria) Johann Mattheson also discussed national traits and taste. The first chapter ("On the Differences Between Today's Italian, French, English, and German Music") contains information about North-German attitudes toward music produced in other countries. The discussion owes something to Ragunet's Parallèle des Italiens et des Français (1702). The excerpt below also reveals Mattheson's confident tone, a notable difference from Addison's discussion of music in Spectator 29:

> The Italians, who today take the prize above all other nations--partially through the inherent beauty of their work, partially also through their subtle and facile artfulness in composition...and who most often have the general taste on their side, differ in style not only from the French, Germans and English but in certain pieces even amongst themselves. 25

On the basis of this statement, taste in music seems to have been characterized by beauty and compositional prowess. Yet taste is not quite the same thing as style, since style is hardly universal in nature. Mattheson expands on this in the next paragraphs, noting that nowhere "throughout the entire world is music in so many various types and ways, and with such success, as it is in Italy."[26] Mattheson also observes that "only because a large part of such things depend upon taste does French music not have as yet the same approbation in the world as the French language."[27] To Mattheson taste was a part of the critical process:

> If one wished to briefly summarize the topic discussed and compare the nations with one another, so might one proceed: the Italians execute the best; the French entertain the best; the Germans compose and work the

> best; and the English judge the best. The first make themselves admirable; the second aimiable; the third indefatigable; and the fourth equitable. The first are ingenius; the second spiritual; the third fundamental; and the fourth delicate. The first uplift music; the second enliven it; the third seek after it; and the the fourth give it its rightful due. The first serve music; the second make company with it; the third anatomize it; and the fourth are served by it. The first have much invention, but little industry; and the second industry but not their best; the third have much invention and great industry; the fourth have the best Goût. 28

To Mattheson excellence in composition and performance did not guarantee that the music was tasteful. If it did, Mattheson continues, the British could not possibly be said only to be the best judges of music but also to have the best taste. Taste and judgement seem to be removed from actual musical practice and depended on qualities in the listener. In any event, Mattheson regarded the British very highly, more highly than British music of the early eighteenth century deserved. These excerpts may actually show Mattheson's admiration for British thinkers. One wonders if his own translation of numbers from Tatler and Spectator, as well as his association with the Wich family in Hamburg, helped to arouse this admiration.

Taste in the 1720s

Though Alexander Malcolm made it clear on the first page of his work that he knew Shaftesbury and was encouraged by him to write the Treatise, he did not find the term taste as attractive as Shaftesbury had.[29] He used the term only once, during his discussion of ancients and moderns:

> Yet perhaps it will be replied, That this [i.e., approval of modern composers] proceeds from a bad Taste, and something natural, in applauding the best thing we know of any Kind. 30

This comment reminds one of that made later by Francis Hutcheson, that "bad Musick pleases Rusticks who have never heard any better,"--the argument here being that we can have only as much taste as we have experience.[31] From this statement it seems safe to infer that Malcolm's attitude toward taste was not much different from that of Hutcheson's or Shaftesbury's, though the ambiguity of the term may have made him uncomfortable.

Taste is a term Roger North used two ways. The first emphasizes the idea that music of "bon goust" is not appropriate for representing meditative states:

> But where heads are brisk and airey hunting of entertainments, and brought to musick as the best, where it is expected to be accordingly, and the audititors have not leisure or patience to attend moderate things, but must be touched sensibly, brisk, and with bon goust; then I confess this sort of thing [i.e., soft viol music] will not please. 32

North broadens his use of the term in his "The Judgement of Musick" (c. 1726). Here he deals with that aspect of "taste as judgement" which other British writers (especially Addison) found so fascinating. In his discussion of the music of the ancients and moderns North asks "Must wee resort then to the generall gusto? That's yet worse; for as our taste will not bear the Antique manner, so it's probable the Ancients would not have borne ours."[33] North regards taste as a quality which has changed from the time of the ancients, and suggests that taste was something which was not inborn, but developed. Similarly, the general taste was something shared by many individuals--perhaps in other countries as well. Unfortunately, North does not go further, and though the basic concept of taste as a factor of aesthetic judgement is touched on, he never qualifies his remarks.

James Ralph presents the historian with the opposite problem: he used the term in numerous ways that it is difficult to define exactly what it meant to him. We read, for example, of "the vitious Taste of the Town," "bad Taste," "elegant Taste," "exquisite Goû," "picquant Goû," the "British Taste," the "Taste, even of the Dregs of the People," and so forth.[34] Despite the variety of usages, Ralph, like Addison, seems to have regarded the term as being caught up in the process of artistic judgement. Thus, just as a theater has higher and lower seats, it holds an audience of higher and lower tastes.[35] The faculty of judgement, which Ralph felt varied among men, could be improved--indeed, this opinion prompted him to write his work.

Ralph's discussions of taste and music present some interesting attitudes. First, musical tastes differ from country to country. After a long discussion of the possibility for acceptable British operas, Ralph adds: "I have made my Remarks on this Head the more full, in hopes that the Hints advanced here, might of themselves accommodate our Italian Operas to the British Taste and Ears."[36] Ralph found the opera house to be the focal point of aesthetic discussion (and social posturing) and discussed not only British opera, but French and Italian as well. French opera seems to have been especially difficult for Ralph, who noted that "though I have been often an auditor and sometimes a Performer in French Musick, I can neither describe, nor give any Man, that has not heard it, a tolerable Idea of it."[37] Ralph seemed confident he could "accomodate Italian Operas to British Taste and Ears," but to do the same for French opera seems to have been an impossibility.

Johann Mattheson's attitude toward taste matured in the 1720s. The term is not used indiscriminately as it was in his earlier writings. Most frequent is the use of the term _abgeschmackt_ (in poor taste), usually in passages of severe condemnation.[38] Good taste remains an important concept, however, and references to it are common, especially in _Critica Musica_, the most commercial of his writings. During the 1720s Mattheson devoted some time to the discussion of innate ideas. He had problems with this concept, and commented on the expression _de gustibus enim disputandum non est_:

> This axiom seems to be losing its strength, because when one reflects, certain grounds for a right and healthy taste (which one takes _proprie_ or _figurate_) can be given so that they are beyond dispute for all rational people; even though here and there many _dissentientes_ can be found. 39

Here Mattheson casts aside any attempt to embrace Locke's attitudes toward innate ideas, and rejects one of the basic tenets of British empiricism.[40] Like Wolff, Mattheson masquerades as an empiricist, but did not have the humility to be one.

Heinichen also devoted considerable time to the concept of taste in music, making so many references to taste in the introduction to Der General-Baß that one is reminded of Mattheson's efforts a decade before. The importance of good taste in music is, to Heinichen, inestimable, though he adds that it "allows itself so little to be described as the actual being of the soul."[41] Heinichen's appreciation for the importance of taste is coupled with a belief that even a great talent "must first be purified in the fire of experience before it grows into a solid mass, I mean into a well-cultivated and permanent taste."[42] He makes it clear that, though invention is inborn, "taste must be regulated, and this we must do first through industry and experience."[43] Composers who lack this refined taste will be poor ones.

For Heinichen the concept of taste was much involved with mixing the contrapuntal and homophonic styles, and he notes that "one must attempt to temper wooden counterpoint with things of taste."[44] Here one also sees the conflict between the contrapuntal and theatrical styles. One is reminded of J. A. Scheibe, whose objections to the music of J. S. Bach were based on similar attitudes. Heinichen presents the dilemma of the early eighteenth-century composer in the following fashion:

> How many things could be written about the practice of musical taste, invention, accompaniment, of their nature, differences and affect; yet no one wants to investigate those materials necessary for the Praxim sublimiorem, or provide the slightest introduction to it; yet great quantities of useless rules are thought up for pedantic materials. Yes indeed, because even in our time we do not wish to believe that these still strange materials can be given rules or introduction; so we set up our studies blindly on pure eye-music, and hold only those compositions most beautiful where paper

> art [i.e., intricate polyphony] holds the sceptor while [that music] whose art must be provided by taste, brilliance, and a number of rules of experience, is perversly despised. To this latter class belongs mainly the <u>stylus theatralis</u>, and it will be allowed one here to contribute something toward an evaluation of it. 45

Throughout <u>Der General-Baß</u>, Heinichen maintained that the theatrical style was the type of music which required the most taste to compose. In a discussion of the theatrical style he noted that, not only should one mix different affections into a given aria, but extreme states of emotion, such as "black melancholy", should be avoided.[46] As Richard Tanner pointed out sixty-eight years ago, these remarks are of extreme importance in understanding Heinichen's approach to composition.[47] Not only does such an attitude fit well into the aesthetic of the new <u>style galant</u>, but it also explains why Heinichen's music seems somewhat colorless to us today.[48] This is a good example of how concern for a particular aesthetic concept, in this case taste, can affect a composer's entire output.

Like Heinichen, Baron viewed taste as an innate quality, but one which had to be developed through experience:

> If we thoroughly investigated wherein the best taste is found, we could only say that it is "an understanding sharpened through much practice and experience in a given art, one with which a person can grasp all the contributing details without self-interest or prejudice and assess the quality of it according to the proportion of its value." This task in the arts is only to be found among noble and cultivated minds. 49

An important part of taste was also to be found in the proper appreciation of national styles. Baron made it

clear that the galant artist must also be an artist of taste, and recognize the new Italianate manner. Like Addison and Mattheson, Baron compared the musical tastes of Italy, France and Germany, and then noted that "every nation has something special in its music, and it is best to assemble the particularly outstanding elements of each and apply them to one's own ends. A galant artist must not be narrow, but rather should be able to change himself like a chameleon."[50]

Baron's discussion of taste and the galant artist reflects the continued interest in grace and refinement during the 1720s. Most importantly, his discussion of taste reveals the overwhelming importance the concept had to musicians and audiences of his day. Baron even cites Gracian (as had Addison and Mattheson) to support his arguments on several matters concerning taste.[51] His work is remarkable, however, in the attention he paid not just to the tastes of the audience (taste as judgement) but the taste of the virtuoso himself (taste in performance).

Taste in the 1730s

In his dedication to Colonel Blathwayt in the Method, John Frederick Lampe speaks of his patron's "elegant Taste," a quality placed first in a long list of the Colonel's personal attributes.[52] Unfortunately, he never expanded upon the term itself, and it does not appear with any frequency in either of his writings of the decade. At least in this instance, Darenberg's comment that Lampe brought little new to the discussion of aesthetic matters seems justified.[53] It should also be noted that the term itself is less frequently encountered in the 1730s.

Lampe's remark in The Art of Musick that art improves nature "in the Expression and Taste" may reveal a debt to Addison. Both men felt that taste was a quality of judgement excercised by the artist involved.[54]

Because of their complexity, before examining Scheibe's specific definitions of taste a general picture of his attitude toward the term must be presented. Like Addison and Ralph, Scheibe wished to write about music not only to inform his readers, but to improve their taste.

> When I said I would look only to good taste, this was my opinion: I would trouble myself to lead all my readers, be they what they may, to good taste, including those who otherwise would not interest themselves in music, and give them reasonable definitions of good taste and the truly beautiful in music in my pages. 55

Despite this statement, one does not encounter the term with any frequency in Scheibe's writings. His caution with the use of the term may have been the result of Gottsched's struggle to deal more effectively with it, and also the increasing popularity of other terms (such as Witz) with which one might describe characteristics of persons or things subjectively. One manifestation of this sensitivity was Scheibe's opinion that one should not speak of national tastes in music, but national styles.[56] Scheibe makes it clear that while styles differ from nation to nation, good taste remains a constant. "Good taste is, then, general, but style has its differences in music as well as in other sciences," he notes, adding "one confuses style not only with thought, but also with taste and the method to play and sing."[57] While Scheibe's differentiation between taste and style is an interesting one, his lists of national traits of the French, Italians, Germans, and Poles are

quite unoriginal. Since Mattheson and others used the term taste interchangably with style, Scheibe's clarification, though well-intentioned, did not prove helpful in his own attempts to define what taste actually was.

Much has been written about Scheibe's definition of taste as "an ability of the understanding to judge what the senses experience."[58] Both Wilheim and Birke have taken Scheibe to task for the inconsistencies of his supporting arguments and for his confusion about the difference between sense cognition and understanding.[59] Before discussing this, however, it might be helpful to examine the definition of taste set forth by his teacher, Gottsched:

> Taste, in poetry, is a readiness to judge properly the beauty of a poem, thought or expression, which one has for the most part only perceived clearly, but which one has not tested with the rules. It is either good--if it coincides with the rules which are already strongly set in poetics by reason--or bad--if it is the product of the senses, judged without rules, and thus betrays the sensual judgement. 60

Gottsched's definition reveals his study of Leibniz, who had differentiated between four levels of knowledge: "(1) obscure and confused knowledge, resulting from perceived yet unrecognized sensations as occur in a dream, (2) clear but confused knowledge, where we are aware of and attentive to phenomena without defining them, (3) distinct knowledge, which permits definition, and finally, (4) adequate knowledge, where previously unconscious, obscure and confused awareness has risen to a conscious and distinct representation."[61] In this scheme, aesthetic knowledge occupies the second level--that is, clear but confused knowledge which approaches instinct.[62]

Scheibe presents two definitions of taste, the first of which, in Critischer Musicus, is considered by Birke to be the better.[63] Here Scheibe maintains that taste is the actual judgement, not the ability to judge. His opinion that taste is the combination of proper sense experience and proper intellectual understanding is in keeping with the views of other musical writers we have examined in this study. Though his definition of taste as "an ability of the understanding to judge those things which the senses experience" confuses the difference between judgement of the intellect and that of the senses (as Birke has pointed out), we can praise his desire to clarify the meaning of the term. As Birke said, "pioneering efforts, which can scarcely build on previous efforts (one thinks of Gottsched's Dichtkunst) are seldom free of shortcomings."[64]

In his essay on recitative from 1745, Scheibe makes special reference to Addison's remarks on the "general Sense and Taste of Mankind." Scheibe agreed with Addison that there were universal laws of taste which were common to all the arts--an idea which appealed to Scheibe's desire to create a system of music universal in scope.[65] Scheibe also seems to have felt that taste was an innate quality, which he supported with his arguments about national styles as opposed to national tastes. His attempts to clarify taste, and restrict the use of the word to certain situations were laudable, but unsuccessful. Like Addison, however, he did attempt to improve the taste of his readers and, by citing him, provides the modern historian with another link between British and German musical thought.

Lorenz Mizler evidently considered taste a variable factor, not an innate quality, and was less interested in defining the term itself. In his preface to his Fux translation Mizler noted that "the basis of composition remains unaltered, taste may change as it will."[66] His defense of Fux in this preface reveals Mizler's dislike for the tastes of his day, perhaps an indication why he used the term rarely, and then in the context of criticism. The realm of taste, which was looked upon by many as an area of clear but confused knowledge (to use Leibniz's categories), was seen by Mizler as inappropriate in discussions of the musical art. Because discussions of the new galant style so frequently used the term, Mizler may have seen connotations in it not in keeping with his own attitudes toward music.

Johann Mattheson's discussion of taste in the 1730s shows some important differences from his previous writings. Most obvious is his emphasis on tastefulness in melodic ornamentation.[67] Perhaps more important for our purposes was Mattheson's decision that it was impossible to give rules on taste--a turn-around from his attitude in the previous decade. Significantly, his new stance is revealed in a citation from Rameau during a discussion on melody:

> Melody is no less forceful than harmony, but it is almost impossible to give fixed rules on it, since good taste plays a greater part than the rest. 68

The inclusion of this remark indicates that Mattheson felt taste was beyond literal definition, though its participation in the creative process, not simply judgement of art, was required. Was Mattheson advocating a strict Lockean position, that there were no innate ideas? The answer to this question is revealed in Mattheson's later writings. Scheibe, who had criticized what he considered Mattheson's over-emphasis of the sensual aspect of taste, was answered by Mattheson several years later in Die neueste Untersuchung der Singspiele, nebst beygefügter musikalischen Geschmacks-Probe (Hamburg, 1744). Disagreeing with Scheibe's contention that taste was the unifying element between the intellectual and sensual, and could be "defined," Mattheson maintained that "taste indeed examines and judges; but one cannot make final conclusions."[69] Siegfried Kross has pointed out that Mattheson never succumbed to the "rationalistic euphoria" which led Gottsched and Scheibe to extend such an importance to the concept of taste.[70] Actually, one might say that Mattheson rejected this "euphoria" only after he himself had flirted with it in the previous decades.

1 Ernest Tuveson, "Shaftesbury and the Age of Sensibility," in Studies in Criticism and Aesthetics, 1660-1800: Essays in Honor of Samuel Holt Monk (Minneapolis: University of Minnesota Press, 1967).

2 Thomas B. Gilmore, Jr., Early Eighteenth-Century Essays on Taste (Delmar, New York: Scholars' Facsimiles and Reprints, 1972), xvii.

3 Alexander von Bormann, Vom Laienurteil zum Kunstgefühl (Tübingen, 1974), 4.

4 Lewis White Beck, Early German Philosophy (Cambridge: Harvard University Press, 1969), 496.

5 Monroe Beardsley, Aesthetics from Classical Greece to the Present (New York: Macmillan, 1966), 180.

6 Hannelore Klein, There is no Disputing about Taste. Untersuchung zum englischen Geschmacksbegriff im Achtzehnten Jahrhundert (Münster: Aschendorf, 1967), 1.

7 Rémy Saisselin, Taste in Eighteenth Century France. Critical Reflections on the Origins of Aesthetics; or, An Apology for Amateurs (Syracuse: Syracuse University Press, 1965), 47-48.

8 See A. Bosker, Literary Criticism in the Age of Johnson (Groningen: J. B. Wolters, 1930), 20.

9 Gilmore, Essays, iii.

10 Ibid., vii.

11 J. E. Spingarn, Critical Essays of the Seventeenth Century (Oxford: Clarendon Press, 1908), I, xc.

12 Gilmore, Essays, 172.

13 Ibid., 172-173.

14 W. P. Ker, Essays of John Dryden (Oxford: Oxford University Press, 1926), II, 7.

15 Bormann, Kunstgefühl, 4.

16 Werner Weisbach, Vom Geschmack und seinen Wandlungen (Basel: Amerbach, 1947), 26.

17 Ibid., 26-27.

18 J. J. Quantz, Versuch einer Anweisung die Flöte traversiere zu spielen, trans. by Oliver Strunk in Source Readings in Music History (New York: Norton, 1950), 580.

19 Beck, Early German Philosophy, 496.

20 Weisbach, Geschmack, 18-19.

21 Saisselin, Taste, 132.

22 Joseph Addison and Richard Steele, The Spectator, ed. by Donald Bond (London: Clarendon Press, 1965), I, 121.

23 Ibid., I, 122.

24 Ibid., I, 123.

25 Johann Mattheson, Das neu-eröffnete Orchestre (Hamburg, 1713), 200ff: Die Italiäner, welche heutiges Tages, theils durch die wesentliche Schönheit ihrer Wercke, theils auch durch die übertünchte und insinuante Kunst-Griffe in der Composition, den Preis vor allen andern Nationen davon zu tragen scheinen, und den generalen Goût mehrentheils auff ihrer Seiten haben, sind nicht nur in ihrem Stylo von den Frantzosen, Teutschen und Engelländern; sondern in gewissen Stücken unter sich selbst mercklich unterschieden.

26 Ibid., 204-205: Woraus denn erhellet, daß in keinem noch bekannten Lande in der gantzen Welt, die Music so häuffig, auf so mancherley Art und Weise, und mit solchem Success als in Italien exculiret und aestimiret werde.

27 Ibid., 208: Allein weil ein grosses Theil in solchen Sachen von dem Goût deprendiret, und aber die Frantzosen noch keine solche generale Approbation ihrer Music, als wol ihrer Sprache, in der Welt erhalten haben.

28 Ibid., 219-220: Wolte man nun das obenberührte kurz zusammen fassen, und die Nationes eine gegen die andere halten, so möchte man überhaupt und unmassgeblich setzen: Die Italianer executiren am besten; (durchgehends davon zu

reden) die Frantzosen divertiren am besten; die Teutschen aber componiren und arbeiten am besten; und die Engelländer judiciren am besten. Die Ersten machen sich admirables; die Andern aimables; die Dritten infatigables, und die Vierten equitables. Die Ersten sind ingenieuz; die Andern spirituels; die Dritten fondamentels, und die Vierten delicats. Die Erste erheben die Music; die Andern beleben sie; die Dritten bestreben sich darnach, und die Vierten geben was rechtes davor. Die Ersten dienen der Music; die Andern machen eine Compage daraus; die Dritten anatomiren sie; und den Vierten dienet sie. Die Ersten haben viel Invention, wenden aber mit Fleiß wenig Fleiß und die andern den ihren nicht zum besten an; die Dritten haben viel Invention und ungemeinen Fleiß, die Vierten aber den besten Goût.

29 Alexander Malcolm, A Treatise of Music: Speculative, Practical, and Historical (Edinburgh, 1721), xix.

30 Ibid., 589.

31 Francis Hutcheson, An Inquiry into the Origin of our Ideas of Beauty and Virtue (2nd ed.; London, 1726), 66.

32 John Wilson, Roger North on Music: Being a Selection from his Essays written during the years c.1695-1728 (London: Novello, 1959), 11.

33 Ibid., 290-291.

34 James Ralph, The Touchstone: or, Historical, Critical, Political, and Theological Essays on the reigning Diversions of the Town (London, 1728), 84, 136, 174, 222, 31, and 70.

35 Ibid., 138.

36 Ibid., 150.

37 Ibid., 39.

38 Johann Mattheson, Critica Musica (Hamburg, 1722-1725), I, 20, 76, 98, 100, 211n.

39 Ibid., II, 255-255n: Dieses Axioma scheinet seine Kraft nach gerade zu verliehren, weil wenn man es wohl nachdenket, ganz gewiss unumstössliche Grunde von einem

rechten gesunden Geschmack (man nehme ihn proprie oder figurate) gegeben werden können, so dass dieselbe bey allen vernunftigen ausser Dispüt seyn mögen; obgleich hie und da viele dissentientes gefunden werden. bey andrer Gelegenheit ein mehrers hievon.

40 Beck, Early German Philosophy, 267.

41 Johann David Heinichen, Der General-Baß in der Composition (Dresden, 1728), 22n-23n: Was Goût in der Musik heisse, brauchet wohl bey Musicverständigen keini Erklärung, und lässet essentialiter eben so wenig beschreiben, als das eigentliche Wesen der Seelen.

42 Ibid., 23n-24n: Denn auch das aller Invention-reichste Naturell oder Talent gleichet an sich selbst nur einer rohen Gold und Silber-reichen schlacken, welche erstlich durch das Feuer der Erfahrung, wohl muss gereiniget werden, ehe sie zu einer soliden Massa, ich meine zu einem wohl cultivirten, und beständigen Goût gedeyen kan.

43 Ibid., 24n: Der Goût muss sie [die Invention] reguliren, und diesen müssen wir uns erst durch Fleiss viel, und offt schwere Erfahrungs-Regeln zu Wege bringen.

44 Ibid., 25n: ...so bleibet es dabey, mann muss die an sich selbst höltzernen Contrapuncte zu temperiren, und mit Sachen von Goût abzuwechseln suchen...

45 Ibid., 25: Was lese sich nicht practice von musicalischen Goût, Invention, accompagnement, deren Natur, Unterschied und Würckung schreiben; allein niemand will dergleichen ad Praxim sublimiorem abziehlende Materien untersuchen, oder die geringste Anleitung hierzu geben; Da hingegen von anderen Offt pedantischen Materien gantze Fuder unnützer Regeln erdacht worden. Ja eben des wegen, weil wir bey unsern Zeiten noch nicht einmahl glauben wollen, dass man in dergleichen uns noch frembden Materien, Anleitung oder Regeln geben könne; so richten wir blindlings unsere meiste Studia auff pure Augen-Music, und halten nur die jenigen Compositiones, wo pappierne Künste das Scepter führen, vor die schönsten; diejenigen aber verachten wir verkehrter Weise, wo Goût, Brilliant, und die Menge schwehrer Erfahrungs Regeln ihre Künste erweisen müssen. Zu der letztern Classe gehöret hauptsächlich der

Stylus Theatralis, und wird mir erlaubet seyn, alhier zu seiner Desencion etwas beyzutragen.

46 Ibid., 47n-48n: Also, wird man v. g. bey einer verliebten Melancholie, eher die angenehme Liebe, als die schwarze Melancholie zu expirmiren trachten.

47 Richard Tanner, Johann David Heinichen als dramatischer Komponist: Ein Beitrag zur Geschichte der Oper (Leipzig: Breitkopf & Härtel, 1916), 14.

48 Ibid., 14.

49 Ernst Gottlieb Baron, Untersuchung des Instruments der Lauten (Nuremberg, 1727), 147; trans. by Douglas Alton Smith (Redondo Beach, California: Instrumenta Antiqua, 1976), 174: Wolte man aber überhaupt untersuchen worinnen der beste Gusto bestünde, so kan man nicht anders sagen, als daß "ein durch viele Practique und Erfahrung in gewisser Kunst geschärffter Verstand sey, dadurch man alle darein sich concentrirende Umstände gantz ohne Eigennutz und Vor-Urtheil einsehen und das Gute davon nach Proportion seines Werthes schätzen kan.

50 Ibid., 148; 174: Eine jede Nation hat etwas besonders in ihrer Music, und ist das beste, wenn man alles dasjenige was eine jede en particulier besonders hat, zusammen nimmt, und solches zu seinem Endzweck anwendet. Man muss in solchen galanten Künsten nicht wie ein Schuster bey seinem Leist bleiben, sondern darinnen wie das Thier Chameleon sich verändern können.

51 Ibid., 156; 184.

52 John Frederick Lampe, A Plain and Comprehensive Method of Teaching Thorough Bass (London, 1737), ii.

53 Karl Darenberg, Studien zur englischen Musikaesthetik des 18. Jahrhunderts (Hamburg: Cram-de Gruyter, 1960), 53.

54 John Frederick Lampe, The Art of Musick (London, 1740), 6.

55 Johann Adolph Scheibe, Critischer Musicus (Hamburg, 1738), 43, 135: Wenn ich also gesaget habe, ich würde lediglich auf den guten Geschmack sehen: so ist meine Meynung gewesen: Ich wurde mich bemühen alle Leser sie

mögten auch seyn, wie sie wollten, auf den guten Geschmack zu leiten: Dass also auch diejenigen, welche sich sonst eben nicht um die Music bekummern, moralische und vernünftige Begriffe vom guten Geschmacke und von dem wahren Schönen in der Music aus meinen Blättern erhalten sollen.

56 Johann Adolph Scheibe, Compendium Musices (Leipzig, 1736), 85.

57 Scheibe, Critischer Musicus, 12, 95:Der gute Geschmack ist also allgemein, die Schreibart aber hat ihren Unterschied in der Music sowohl als in andern Wissenschaften.; 12, 98: Man verwechselt die Schreibart nicht nur mit dem Denken, sondern auch mit dem Geschmack und mit der Methode zu singen und spielen.

58 Ibid., 2nd. ed., 767: Der Geschmack ist eine Fähigkeit des Verstandes, dasjenige zu beurtheilen, was die Sinne empfinden.

59 Immanuel Wilheim, "J. A. Scheibe: German Musical Thought in Transition" (Ph.D. dissertation, University of Illinois, 1963), 114-119; Joachim Birke, Christian Wolffs Metaphysik und die zeitgenössische Literatur- und Musiktheorie: Gottsched, Scheibe, Mizler (Berlin: de Gruyter, 1966), 64-66.

60 Johann Christian Gottsched, Handlexikon oder kurzgefaßtes Wörterbuch der schönen Wissenschaften und freyen Künste (Leipzig, 1760), 759-760: Geschmack, in der Poesie, ist eine Fertigkeit, von der Schönheit eines Gedichtes, Gedankens oder Ausdruckes recht zu urtheilen; die man grösstentheils nur klar empfunden, aber nach den Regeln selbst nicht geprüfet hat. Er ist entweder gut, wenn er mit den Regeln überein kömmt, die von der Vernunft, in der Dichtkunst allbereit fest gesetzet worden; oder übel, wenn er nach der blossen Empfindung ohne Regeln urtheilet; aber sich in solchen seinen Urtheilen betrügt.

61 Wilheim, "Scheibe," 112.

62 K. Gilbert and H. Kuhn, eds., A History of Aesthetics (New York: Macmillan, 1939), 228.

63 Birke, _Wolff_, 64.

64 Ibid., 66.

65 Scheibe, _Critischer Musicus_, 1, 8.

66 J. J. Fux, _Gradus ad Parnassum_, trans. by Lorenz Mizler (Leipzig, 1742), 2: Der Grund der Setzkunst bleibet unverrückt, es mag sich der Geschmack ändern, wie er will.

67 Johann Mattheson, _Der vollkommene Capellmeister_ (Hamburg, 1728), 110, 130, 130; trans. by Ernest C. Harriss (Ann Arbor: UMI Research Press, 1981), 265, 295, 295.

68 Ibid., 136-137n; 305, 488n: La Melodie n'a pas moins de force dans les expressions que l'Harmonie, mais il est presque impossible de pouvoir en donner des regles certaines, en ce que le bon gout y a plus de part que le reste.

69 See Siegfried Kross, "Mattheson und Gottsched," in _New Mattheson Studies_, ed. by George Buelow and Hans Joachim Marx, (New York: Cambridge University Press, 1983), 341.

70 Ibid., 327-344.

CHAPTER VII

MUSIC AND "IMAGINATION" IN THE AGE OF REASON

One of the most intriguing issues of the period under examination is that of the concept of the imagination. The issue has been made more complex in the last hundred years by historians anxious to write about "The Age of Reason" or "The Classic Period". Certainly, there was strong regard for reason as the preferred guiding factor in the lives of all men between 1700 and 1750. Even so, it is not fair to maintain that--as one recent writer impishly phrases the conventional view--early eighteenth-century men "retired to garrets to write rational essays and couplets on practical matters of town life."[1] If anything, the age was one in which "the passions" were regarded as the primary forces of life. Reason was considered the guide needed to focus them.

An example of the importance of imagination to writers even before 1700 can be seen in Descartes's definition of it in Passions of the Soul:

> [Imaginings which have the body alone as their cause] come about owing to the manner in which the spirits (variously agitated and coming upon traces of diverse impressions which have preceded them in the brain) take their course fortuitously by certain pores rather than by others. Such are the illusions of our dreams and the daydreams we often have when awake. 2

Descartes and later writers had difficulty expressing their thoughts on the imagination. For writers on all the arts the concept of the imagination represented an important but vague component in any kind of aesthetic system. The "pleasures of the imagination" were widely praised, but never discussed in great detail. Even today the matter of just how definitions of the imagination affected eighteenth-century writers has yet to be dealt with successfully. Though it is beyond the scope of this work to present such an analysis, a few points relevant to this study are commented upon, providing the background necessary for understanding the use of the term in musical writings examined in this chapter.

Theories of Imagination in France, Britain, and Germany

Nicolas Boileau's L'art poétique of 1674 made him famous as a literary theorist who spoke out for refinement in form and expression. Perhaps this couplet from Dryden's translation of his work presents Boileau's attitude best:

> Love reason, then: and let what e'er you write
> Borrow from her its Beauty, Force, and Light. 3

Another work by Boileau was also extremely popular at the turn of the century. His translation of Longinus's _On the Sublime_ presented the view that in 'sublime' poetry a strong emotional response on the part of the reader was of critical importance. It was one of the ironies of the age that the same writer who advocated moderation in expression provided, through his translation, an intellectual basis for a movement that had little use for the platitudes of the _Académie_.

Britain provided the most fertile ground for the thoughts of Boileau-Longinus. British literature already had a tradition which depended upon the fancy and imagination of the writer and reader. Even the phrase "pleasures of the imagination," an expression made popular by Joseph Addison, came to be identified with such figures as Shakespeare and Milton.[4] The concept of the sublime was not a movement with as strong a French bias as taste had been. British writers (especially Addison and Shaftesbury) devoted considerable time to discussion of the sublime. Addison described the "pleasures of the imagination" as arising "from visual objects, either when we have them actually in our view, or when we call up their ideas into our minds by paintings, statues, descriptions, or any like occasion."[5] For Addison, the first category involved pleasures caused by "a pleasing astonishment at such unbounded views."[6] The second were those pleasures given by the arts. Even in music "there may be confused, imperfect notions of this nature raised in the imagination by an artificial composition of notes."[7]

Addison's description of the imagination and its importance was combined with a nationalistic pride in British writers:

> Among all the poets of this kind our English are the best, by what I have seen, whether it be that we abound with more stories of this Nature, or that the Genius of our Country be fitter for this sort of Poetry. For the English are naturally Fanciful, and very often disposed to that Gloominess and melancholly of Temper, which is so frequent in our Nation, to many wild Notions and Visions to which others are not so liable. 8

Unlike other nationalistic prejudices popular at that time, Addison's opinion about the unusually high number of imaginative British writers was shared by many continental thinkers (especially in Germany and Switzerland). Addison's writings on the imagination came into vogue on the continent and, along with empiricism, became one of the major ideas to come out of Britain during the first half of the century.

Theories on the powers of the imagination played an important role in the outlooks of both literary and philosophical writers in Germany. Although concepts of the imagination flew in the face of rationalistic doctrine there was a great interest in them. This interest was heightened by discussions of literary critics, but philosophical investigations and well-established precedents set by the rhetorical tradition were also of importance. Because of the complexity of these interrelationships some of them will be discussed here in detail. These literary, philosophical, and rhetorical aspects to the concept were all important to early eighteenth-century German writers on music.

The most famous example of the importance of the concept of the imagination to German writers before 1750 is the debate that went on between J. C. Gottsched and the Swiss writers, Bodmer and Breitinger.[9] Gottsched wielded considerable power from his position as lecturer at the University of Leipzig. The conflict between these men manifested itself most obviously in Breitinger's attack on Gottsched (even though the latter is not mentioned by name) in his Critische Dichtkunst (1740). This disagreement can be seen in a variety of ways, as Lewis White Beck has pointed out: as a conflict between French literary theory (Gottsched) and that of England (the Swiss); as the conflict between an aesthetic based on *a priori* rules and one on *a posteriori* experience; or even as "the struggle between academic art and an anarchistic aesthetic of unregulated emotion."[10] Though Gottsched followed the latter view, it was actually the only truly false one. Bodmer and Breitinger were not anarchists, and did place considerable importance on method and rules. It was in the great emphasis placed by the Swiss upon the imagination, often discussing the eminence of Milton and Shakespeare, that they differed most from the Gottsched. Even more important than their disagreement, however, was the impact these men had on German intellectuals, particularly J. A. Scheibe.

German philosophy also addressed the issue of the imagination and in doing so made an important contribution to the study of the arts. Christian Wolff presented a system of thought where only the higher cognitive faculty, thought, could be perfect.[11] All sense perception was, by nature, imprecise. The ramifications of Wolff's system were negative for anyone active in the arts, since these activities were also doomed to a certain kind of irrelevancy. Similarly, Wolff's system made little provision for the "lower sensual powers" (*unteres Erkenntnisvermögen*) and a great gap existed in the realm of artistic criticism. This problem was recognized and corrected by A. G. Baumgarten, (Aesthetica, 1740) who maintained that there was a perfection of sense perception itself. As the science of thought is logic, that of the senses was a science which Baumgarten named aesthetics.

In the course of his writings Baumgarten also stressed the concept of the marvellous (das Wunderbare) and recognized the powerful influence of poetry upon an audience. "Stronger impressions are clearer impressions," Baumgarten notes, "therefore it is highly poetic to excite the most powerful affects."[12] There was a place for the wonderful, for imagination in the aesthetics of Baumgarten, and his decision to include both in his writings gave an intellectual basis for those Germans who admired Milton, Shakespeare, and Klopstock.

The Imagination and Rhetoric

As we have already mentioned, there was a strong relationship between the concept the imagination and rhetoric in eighteenth-century Germany. Klaus Dockhorn pointed out some of these relationships over thirty years ago, at that time as a reaction against historians who, in his opinion, had ignored rhetoric as an important field for eighteenth-century studies.[13] Though this seems today to be less the case, few writers have looked seriously at the influence of rhetoric, musical or otherwise, on concepts of the imagination. Normally we immediately associate the art of rhetoric with the concept of the affections, not with the imagination. Yet there is an obvious relationship between the imagination and the inventio, the first step to be taken by the speaker. Here one decides what one will discuss and how one will go about it. According to Gottsched, "to this [the _inventio_] belongs first of all a good imagination [_Erfindungskraft_]: which provides the speaker with the materials, insights, and manner of unifying the parts of his speech."[14] Musical writers saw in the _inventio_ the working stage of a composition--often the choosing of appropriate musical figures to accompany given affections. Maritius Vogt's _Conclave Thesauri Magnae Artis Musicae_ (Prague, 1719), contains a chapter entitled "_De Phantasia et Inventionibus_" which deals with selecting and elaborating fugal themes.[15] Heinichen's and Mattheson's discussion of the _loci topici_ also fall into this general category of rhetorical "imagination."

The tendency of German writers on music in the eighteenth century to involve themselves in discussions of rhetoric makes an appreciation of the _inventio_ important today. Even so, a more far-reaching aspect of the imagination and rhetoric involves the relationship between the art of rhetoric and the affections. John Dennis's comments from _The Advancement and Reformation of Modern Poetry_ (London,1701) illustrate this relationship:

> These passions that attend upon our thoughts are seldom so strong as they are in those kind of thoughts we call images. For they, being the very lively pictures of the things which they represent, set them, as it were, before our eyes. But images are never so admirably drawn as when they are drawn in motion; especially if the motion is violent. For the mind can never imagine violent motion without being in a violent agitation itself; and the imagination being fired with that agitation sets the very things before our eyes, and consequently makes us have the same passions that we should have form the things themselves. For the warmer the imagination is, the more present the things are to us of which we draw the images; and therefore, when once the imagination is so inflamed as to get the

> better of the understanding, there is no difference between the images and the things themselves; as we see, for example, in fear and madmen. 16

As Dockhorn points out, it is important to realize that the ongoing force which rhetoric exerted upon writers like Dennis was linked to a belief in the power of the imagination. Although one might not go so far as Dockhorn and exclude all other considerations, the critical impact of rhetorical thought should not be underestimated.[17] The creative basis for the affections does, after all, hinge upon the concept of the imagination, in this case the imagination of the reader. If the seed of "*vorromantischer Irrationalismus*" is to be found in the world of the affections, the seed of our concept of imagination is likewise found in the early eighteenth century.

Addison and Mattheson on Imagination in the First Decades of the Eighteenth Century

One of Addison's best essays, *Spectator* No. 405, opens with his regrets on the departure of the famous singer Nicolò Grimaldi (1673-1732). Addison expands this farewell into a thoughtful discussion about the nature of music itself:

> Homer and Hesiod intimate to us how this Art [music] should be applied, when they represent the Muses as surrounding Jupiter, and warbling their Hymns about his throne. I might shew, from innumerable Passages in Ancient Writers, not only that Vocal and Instrumental Musick were made use of in their Religious Worship, but that their most favorite Diversions were filled with Songs and Hymns to their respective Deities. Had we frequent Entertainments of this Nature among us, they wou'd not a little purifie and exalt our Passions, give our Thoughts a proper Turn, and cherish those Divine

> Impulses in the Soul, which every one feels that has not stifled them by sensual and immoderate Pleasures. Musick, when thus applied, raises noble Hints in the Mind of the Hearer, and fills it with great Conceptions. It strengthens Devotion, and advances Praise into Rapture. It lengthens out every act of Worship, and produces more lasting and permanent Impressions in the Mind, than those which accompany any transient Form of Words that are uttered in the ordinary Method of Religious Worship. 18

Addison's remarks about the effects of music upon ancient listeners are interesting. If we were exposed to such music, he says, our passions would rise to the point of rapture. Music, then, is capable of raising the passions, but the end result seems to have more to do with Longinus than the concept of the affections. By endowing music with the ability to create rapture Addison makes a connection between music and the concepts of imagination he so successfully developed elsewhere. This connection (expanded upon in Spectator No. 580) had important ramifications for later writers on music who supported Addison's view that music was not just an entertainment, but an art capable of sublime expression.[19] Addison's remark that music makes the "transient Form of Words" more meaningful and memorable is a remarkably positive view from a British writer of that day.

Perhaps the key to understanding Addison's views on music can be found in his attitude toward the imagination. Commenting on music in the church in Spectator No. 580, Addison observes that not only sight, but the other senses would enjoy "their highest Gratifications" in the presence of the Almighty:

> There is nothing which more ravishes and transports the Soul, than Harmony; and we have great Reason to

> believe, from the Descriptions of this Place in Holy Scripture, that this is one of the Entertainments of it. And if the Soul of Man can be so wonderfully affected with those Strains of Musick, which Human Art is capable of production, how much more will it be raised and elevated by those, in which is exerted the whole Power of Harmony! 20

The markedly rhapsodic tone here is maintained throughout No. 580. It seems difficult to reconcile Addison's remarks on opera in Spectator No. 18 as a mere entertainment with those concerning music and religion, and perhaps no reconciliation is necessary. Addison was always somewhat confused and frustrated by an art which he could admire but never understand. Even so, by including music in his discussions throughout the Spectator he managed to initiate a new attitude toward the art. It became, along with the other arts, part of the complex of ideals with which Addison attempted to raise "the cultural and moral standards of his own time."[21] And this is, of course, not only what he set out to do, but what he did do.

Although Johann Mattheson states his views briefly in Das neu-eröffnete Orchestre, one finds fertile ground for later concepts of "sublimity" in art which are often a part of discussions on the imagination. This is particularly evident in the section of the work which deals with the question of which art--music or painting--was superior. Condemning painting as incapable of expressing the highest emotions, Mattheson holds music up as a superior force. Even the actual materials of each of the arts, he says, indicate music's superiority:

> To speak briefly about the actual material of music and painting: it is known that one works with color, the other with sound. Whether to set one before the other, I submit to those who recognize the difference between

> feeling and hearing, which every reasonable and healthy person will do. For color, which one can feel and see, is a mere earthly material and has a quite coarse body; but sound can neither be seen nor felt, but only heard and is therefore, so to speak, not a material thing, but much more, a very spiritual [thing], and properly understood, something incomprehensible. 22

Mattheson presents music not just as a part of nature itself, but an art characterized by a spirituality generated by its own incomprehensibility. Hence, it is an art more suitable than painting for expressing those complex emotions of men which are in themselves beyond sensual comprehension. Mattheson lay the ground work for later German writers on music by acknowledging, as Addison had done, that there was indeed something transcendent in music, which even he, a self-styled enlightener, could not explain.

Imagination in the 1720s

As we have seen in his comments concerning the "new Art" of music and its relation to the affections, Alexander Malcolm was a pioneer in his attitude toward the imagination. Unlike any English-speaking writer on music before him, Malcolm regards the passions as just one aspect of music. Equally important is the impact music has on the mind, a concept caught up in Malcolm's belief (probably borrowed from Hutcheson) that the recognition of unified varieties is a prerequisite to aesthetic enjoyment. In his discussion on musical scales, for example, he observes that variety is "indispensable in our pleasures."[23] That the "Mind is ravished with the Agreement of Things seemingly contrary to one another" and the perception of "the Whole" is a necessary step in appreciating the "new Art" of music, makes Malcolm's comments on the imagination important.[24] The need for this new category of appreciation was created by the inadequacy of the concept of the affections.

Roger North showed considerable interest in the imagination. Throughout his work he stresses the unique importance of "fancy" and "imagination" in music --performance and composition. This attitude leads North to several important conclusions. He doubts, for example, if the study by musicians of rhetoric is helpful, though "the masters of the former affect the methods used by them of the other."[25] North considered music similar to the other sciences, like mathematics, and felt that there must be rules which can explain it better than the imprecise art of rhetoric. He contradicted this opinion, however, when he discussed the elusive nature of music in "What is Ayre?":

> But as for securing an Ayre, if it must be above the indifferent, it is like securing witt in poetry, not to be done; and after all will be found to flow from a genius and not without accidents or rather felicitys of fancy, as well as sound judgement, to make it sublime. 26

The powers of the imagination, according to North, were important in both the creation and enjoyment of music. His skeptical attitude toward those who bring rhetoric into the art of music led him to ask for the creation of an altogether new science, a science of music. It might be mentioned here that North's references to the sublime may have been inspired by the recent <u>Spectator</u> essays on the topic by Addison, notably Nos. 66 and 253.

It is in North's essay on organ voluntaries that he makes most of his remarks concerning the imagination.[27] North lists no fewer than eight requirements which a musician must meet in order to play a good voluntary, and the first requirement was "a genius capable of musick, or what they call an ear." Genius and the inherent musical abilities which make up a good musician occupy an important place in North's view of music.

James Ralph's comments on the imagination also deal with the natural genius of artists, but in the context of criticism. One of the most serious problems with the literary critics of the 1720s, according to Ralph, was their adherence to rules and regulations which are not applicable to the works being examined. This applied to music critics as well. His opinion that opera was a genre which transcended poetic laws seems to echo Addison's remarks on Shakespeare and Milton, both of whom were also considered to be outside the rules by eighteenth-century critics. Although there are no discussions of the creative process in the Touchstone, there is a considerable interest in the sublime. Ralph holds with Addison in describing a particular plot as "English" due to its rustic setting and supernatural overtones. This plot would be perfect for an opera, Ralph notes, because of these characteristics and (it can be assumed) because the story itself could provide an excellent satire of Italian operas. Ralph describes a ballad found in 1719 publication Pills to Purge Melancholy in some detail.[28] The ballad itself, which deals with the combat between a heroic squire and a local dragon, is divided by Ralph into a three-act opera, each act being described in some detail. Ralph notes that "this is an English Story, entirely calculated for the present Set of

Singers, and capable of giving us a vast deal of the Terrible, the distinguishing Characteristicks of Music, as well as Poetry."[29]

What is remarkable about this passage is that it must surely have served as inspiration for Henry Carey's libretto for Lampe, The Dragon of Wantley, set to music and performed in 1737 to great success. Carey follows Ralph's directions very closely, and divides the acts as they are presented in the Touchstone. In addition, the placement of choruses and certain other effects are also taken from Ralph's suggested opera. Frederick T. Wood has pointed this out in his edition of Carey's poems, but no writers on music even touched on this issue until very recently.[30] Unfortunately, any further examination of Ralph's outline is beyond the scope of this study.

The use of the supernatural in opera, which Ralph applauds, seems also to be a part of a general trend toward a support for the sublime in art. One of the charges Ralph leveled at contemporary poets was their neglect of the "true Sublime."[31] Much of this neglect must be ascribed to critics who upheld the authority of literary conventions over that of the sublime, and Ralph's support of the sublime makes his work unusual. Certainly, his works do not deserve the oblivion into which they have fallen.[32] It should also be noted that Ralph's Touchstone was known in the German-speaking world. Gottsched mentions Ralph in the course of his essay on opera in his Critische Dichtkunst, and Ralph's ideas on opera are defended by Lorenz Mizler in his Musikalische Bibliothek. Ralph's interest in the sublime, and the impact of his writings in Germany, deserve more careful study than they have received up to now.

Mattheson's attitude toward the imagination is not consistent in the 1720s. In Das forschende Orchestre he comes as close as he ever does to rejecting its importance, criticizing the mystical platonism of his contemporaries while under the influence of empirical doctrines.[33] In Critica Musica, however, Mattheson upholds the importance of the imagination over "rules" in the making of a good composer. "Genius," he notes, "does the best, the most, yes, almost everything, in the matter; not art, which is nothing more than a handmaiden."[34]

In his advocacy of the power of the imagination Mattheson follows what seems to have been a general trend in the 1720s. He acknowledges the "unbound inspirations" of contemporary composers, whose works exhibit considerable freedom and transcend previously unbreakable rules.[35] Significantly, Mattheson discusses the imagination outside of the context of rhetoric. It would seem that by the 1720s the concept had come into its own.

Though Heinichen did provide, as George Buelow points out, "concrete insights into German compositional principles," he also was interested in less concrete matters.[36] Frequent references are made in Der General-Baß to the imagination, though he does attempt to make concrete even this most incorporeal of subjects with his loci topici. His attitude toward the loci topici was not universally popular, however, and even Mattheson called such devices miserable aids to the composer.[37] Tanner has mentioned the discrepancy between the two men on this issue and places each into a different camp of thought.[38] While the two had their differences, it seems unfair to choose this particular issue as a central point of argument. Even Heinichen was skeptical of the loci topici and pointed out "that this art can give someone true learnedness...must be believed as little as that the _loci topici_ can smear true invention into the mouth of a composer who has from nature no musical talent."[39] It is unfair to portray Heinichen as some kind of "pedant of the imagination"--which is exactly what Mattheson attempted to do (Mattheson probably never really forgave Heinichen for his remarks about the musical circle). In his discussion of the _loci topici_ Heinichen was merely manifesting a profound desire for clarity, as well as the overwhelmingly common tendency of his age to intellectualize the creative process.

The writings of Ernst Gottlieb Baron offer the historian an example of how complex early eighteenth-century attitudes toward the powers of the imagination were. His most detailed discussion on the imagination came during his presentation on playing with good taste. Here he observes that preludes and fantasies were derived from harmonic constructs, usually a single chord.

> I have shown this here so that it can be seen how a single chord can spawn many passages. Now if you add an inventive genius who is more or less profound, then by much permutation and inversion of tones, a good and lovely prelude will necessarily result. 40

Baron had already discussed "Genius on the Lute" in his treatise, devoting an entire chapter to it and noting "if a person wishes to invent something, he must be provided with a good ingenuity." He then compares the capacity for invention to gold ore, which must be "cleansed of its dross, and judgement must be its cleanser."[41]

Baron placed a premium on the musician's ability to guide the natural disposition, or "genius." In his discussion of the fantasy Baron provides his description of the improvising musician. Here Baron points out that even less-gifted musicians can rise to great heights of imagination while playing fantasies--a fact he considers to be a manifestation of natural forces of which we have no real knowledge.[42] This discussion leads Baron to the conclusion that there are in fact innate predilections for art within certain souls, and that instruction alone cannot create a fine composer. Though this idea is nothing new, what is interesting is Baron's fascination with the creative process and his recognition that rules could not deal with it. With this realization Baron goes no further, but observes that "we will do well to respect those people whom God has given special and extraordinary gifts and to promote their welfare."[43]

While positive toward the imagination in the body of his treatise, Baron's work contains an appendix which warns the reader that a too-great attraction toward the irrational can be harmful. Persons of excessive imagination "have their hell on earth and consume themselves in their obscure corners all their lives."[44] At all times in his treatise Baron displays a considerable respect for the power of God, and it is in the context of Baron's religious beliefs that these last remarks should be understood. It would be a mistake to consider Baron a prophet of the irrational, or as a link toward the movement in German arts and letters later in the century which placed such an emphasis on the cult of genius. The imagination was important to Baron, but control of it was also important. For the enlightened musical writer, the two could not be divided.

Imagination in the 1730s

Unfortunately, neither Pepusch nor Lampe discuss the concept of the imagination extensively. While this might be expected from Pepusch, it seems inconceivable that the subject was not of interest to Lampe. There is a passing reference to a kind of creative triad which Lampe envisions as the perfect process of creation in music. We must, Lampe says, fix our minds on the principles of nature, allow ourselves to be inspired by fancy, with "reason assisting to keep due Order and Method."[45]

German publications from the same period reveal more interest in the concept of the imagination. As we have seen in our discussion of his attitude toward the concept of the affections, J. A. Scheibe devoted considerable space in Critischer Musicus to the relationship between music and rhetoric. The inventio of the rhetorical scheme was an important aspect of Scheibe's conception of the compositional process. Although he did not discuss the loci topici in the manner of Heinichen or Mattheson, "certain rules" could be helpful in prodding the imagination of the composer.[46] All of these things are discussed in the context of the capacity for invention as the basis for the musical art.[47] This was very much a part of Scheibe's overall fascination with the inner drive for music, a drive which he felt manifested itself in melody.[48] "Through melody invention expresses itself, " Scheibe said, and maintained the superiority of melody over harmony because of its closeness to the inventive-imaginative process.[49]

Scheibe's interest in the imagination also manifests itself in his discussions of the personal attributes necessary for the ideal composer. "The composer," he wrote, "must possess above all a powerful imagination and a rational memory."[50] No composer can, for example, hope to write convincing music unless he is "fiery and spirited by nature," and the concept of a powerful, fiery imagination as a component of the composer's spiritual make-up is stressed in Scheibe's writings.[51] Still, a fiery imagination alone was not enough.[52] In his hesitancy to allow the imagination a too-free rein, however, Scheibe is similar to many writers of the 1720s and 1730s (notably Baron and Gottsched).

In the second edition of Critischer Musicus Scheibe observed that a composer must regulate his musical expressions according to the quality of the subject matter, being sure to set "sublime and important things" properly.[53] Though the importance of the sublime style in music is an area beyond the scope of this study, Scheibe's footnote to his statement has some bearing on our subject:

> I find an interesting spot in the sixth part of the English Spectator on page 96 of the German translation, which deserves special mention. Addison discusses here the pleasures of the imagination--something which well deserves to be read by a composer, since it belongs to the improvement of the invention. 54

In the excerpt which Scheibe included (Spectator No. 416), Addison comments on the ability of music to re-create certain states of mind or events though these be but indistinct.[55] Addison's point was that music should use this power judiciously, and not abuse it--an attitude Scheibe agreed with wholeheartedly:

> These thoughts [of Addison's] are very favorable, since they take note of the clear difference between true and false expressions. And certainly, an excessive power of imagination has led many immature composers to fall to things which are never expressible, and at the same time are as ridiculous as the artist who attempted to paint the binding formulas of a speech. 56

Scheibe then commented on several compositions, among them Vivaldi's The Seasons, which were, in his opinion, overly programmatic. Although his attitude toward Vivaldi may seem harsh to some, the statement shows an indebtedness to Addison's discussion. Scheibe cited Addison on the subject of the elevated style of church music, noting at one point that "one will read them [Addison's essays] with pleasure, as I myself often have."[57] Of course, Scheibe's enthusiasm was undoubtedly prepared by his reading of Mattheson's works, where he had been exposed (perhaps without knowing) to many of the Briton's ideas long before he set eyes on Frau Gottsched's translations of the Spectator.

Lorenz Mizler's most characteristic comments on the imagination come in the context of another criticism of Gottsched's remarks on opera. Whereas Gottsched maintained that opera was an illogical creation, incapable of imitating nature, Mizler insisted that this was true only for composers who allowed their fantasy too much freedom.[58] In his discussion of odes Gottsched also brings up the imagination, this time to note that the poet must make use of it to reach a level of excitement which Pindar, for example, was said to attain when writing.[59] In his footnote to this remark Mizler merely adds that the musician "in short, must think and write as the poet."[60] Unfortunately, Mizler did not elaborate on this remark.

Mizler also comments on the loci topici, aids to the imagination which Mizler felt were indeed worthwhile. He even reproduced a four-page list of them taken from Mattheson's Capellmeister.[61] Mizler was evidently not as concerned with the artificial nature of the loci topici as he had been with Mattheson's application of rhetorical schemes to the work of Marcello. Mizler's discussion of the imagination reflect his position as a pure theorist, not a performer or composer, and thus are rather dry in comparison to Mattheson's or Heinichen's remarks.

Though Johann Mattheson discussed the loci topici in some detail in his Capellmeister, he "made no great thing out of them," that is, such devices were useful but not substitutes for genius.[62] More interesting are Mattheson's comments concerning the "special type of invention" which Mattheson called inventio ex abrupto or inopinato quasi ex enthusiasmo.[63] Mattheson listed three methods for the excitation of this type of invention:

> 1) If one delves beforehand into the work of an outstanding composer, especially to the extent that he perhaps has dealt with the same sort of material.
>
> 2) If one occupies himself with one affection and as it were, becomes engrossed in it as if one were indeed prayerful, enamored, irate, scornful, melancholy, joyous, etc., this is surely the most certain way to completely unexpected inventions.
>
> 3) If one can also apply diverse inventions in a single melody, and so to speak can almost instantaneously alternate these in an unforseen way: which pleasantly surprises the listeners; if only it does not otherwise interfere with continuity or intent. 64

These three methods of inducing creative thought offer insight into the creative process of Mattheson and other composers of his era. The second method, the admonition to engross oneself in the particular mood which one wishes to reproduce in music, seems logical enough. Few composers of Mattheson's day would have disagreed with him. The final method, geared to producing invention which surprises listeners, seems more descriptive of a C. P. E. Bach keyboard fantasy than a composition of the *style galant*.

Mattheson, the Imagination, and Milton

> Thus it is not true that vocal music is actually and originally older than instrumental: for all sorts of instruments are also ascribed to the angels and saints in the Bible, especially harps and trombones, as string and brass instruments, and they certainly played just as well as they sang before Adam was created. 65

In his critique of Mattheson's *Capellmeister* Lorenz Mizler took time to remark on the above statement by Mattheson which, together with an excerpt from Milton's *Paradise Lost* on a similar topic, are found in the *Vorrede*.[66] "Every reasonable person," Mizler noted "sees himself that God and the blessed spirits have no need of instruments."[67] Those who maintain such a view, Mizler adds, are like those who maintain that angels play on harps and trumpets and point to the works of earthly painters as proof.[68] Mizler's comment reveals the decidedly un-mystical attitudes of a "scientist" in music. Mattheson's remarks could not have received anything but a critical word from Mizler, for he was not only "scientific," he was a student of Gottsched as well. Milton's *Paradise Lost* had been a target for Gottsched's pen on more than one occasion, and the work in general served as a lightning rod for early eighteenth-century literary critics. Bodmer and Breitinger were enthusiastic supporters of Milton's work, and it had been the primary model for Klopstock when writing his epic, Der Messias. Indeed, Klopstock (also disliked by Gottsched) was given the title "the German Milton" by C. F. D. Schubart.[69]

Mattheson's appreciation for the work of Milton is understandable. Fluent in English and an observer of the British literary scene for over thirty years, Mattheson took an interest in the poet that was almost certainly incited by the Spectator essays on Milton by Addison. Mattheson's own religious orientation and love for expansive schemes may also have contributed to his appreciation of Milton, and he probably admired Paradise Lost long before it became stylish in German intellectual circles to do so. It also seems extraordinarily appropriate that Mattheson paid homage to Milton's Paradise Lost in his own "epic," Der vollkommene Capellmeister. Did Mattheson see himself as a "Milton of music?" We may never know, yet his inclusion of a fragment of the poem in his Capellmeister gives the historian an opportunity to examine some of the ideas which both works share.

Many of the mystical concepts which Milton elaborated upon in Paradise Lost, especially those related to music, must have appealed to Mattheson. Milton's elaborate descriptions of the celestial symphony which surrounds the throne of God, and his presentations of the angelic choirs are both poetic renderings of concepts which had, in seventeenth-century writings, fallen under the rubric musica speculativa. Images of universal organs and God as the celestial musician were much a part of the psyche of any musician born late in the seventeenth-century. Kircher's essay in Musurgia universalis which compares the universe to an organ and God to an organist was but one manifestation of such speculative thought.[70] Just as Scheibe was unconsciously prepared for Addison's writings by reading the works of Mattheson, Mattheson was prepared to embrace Milton's mystical and sublime conceptions of music through his own readings of Kircher and writers like him. For all his familiarity with the empirical philosophies of British writers, or his interest in arguments over taste, or the ongoing discussion of the ancients and moderns throughout Europe, Mattheson's attraction toward what was to become known as the "sublime" in Addison's Milton essays was irresistable. That not only Mattheson, but later almost an entire generation of Germans accepted Milton's epic enthusiastically shows the essential truth that in the realm of ideas few things come into the world completely new.

The concept of the sublime in music, and its implicit connection with the power of the imagination, were very much the legacy of Milton and musical writers of the middle Baroque, particularly Kircher (who may have known Milton). Of course, Mattheson founded no school of thought which could be associated with a first step toward musical romanticism, or even musical _Sturm und Drang_. It is a fact, however, that Mattheson's literary tastes were focused on Milton and his eighteenth-century disciple, Addison. Could Mattheson be described as a proto-Romantic in music? To do so seems inappropriate, since it would do violence to the historical realities in which Mattheson should be seen. Mattheson could not have known what would happen in the ensuing decades after the publication of his _Capellmeister_, and it seems doubtful if he would have agreed with many of the tenets of musical romanticism.

Instead, Mattheson's citation of Milton in _Capellmeister_ should be seen as a concrete example of the complexity and pervasiveness of the exchange of ideas between Britain and Germany during the early eighteenth century.

1 A. R. Humphries, *The Augustan World* (London: Methuen, 1954), 189.

2 Rene Descartes, *The Passions of the Soul*, trans. by N. K. Smith in *Descartes Philosophical Writings* (London: Macmillan, 1952), 289.

3 Nicolas Boileau, *The Art of Poetry*, trans by William Soame and John Dryden (London, 1683), 3.

4 Joseph Addison and Richard Steele, *The Spectator*, ed. by Donald Bond (London: Clarendon Press, 1965), III, 536n.

5 Addison, *Spectator*, III, 537.

6 Ibid., III, 540.

7 Ibid., III, 559.

8 Ibid., III, 572.

9 Armand Nivelle, *Kunst- und Dichtungs-Theorien zwischen Aufklärung und Klassik* (Berlin: de Gruyter, 1960), 1.

10 Lewis White Beck, *Early German Philosophy* (Cambridge, Mass.: The Belknap Press of the Harvard University Press, 1969), 281.

11 Ibid., 283ff.

12 Alexander Baumgarten, *Meditationes philosophicae de nonnullus ad poema pertinentibus*, trans. by Karl Aschenbrenner and William Hother (Los Angeles: University of California Press, 1954), 48.

13 Klaus Dockhorn, "Die Rhetorik als Quelle des vorromantischen Irrationalismus in der Literatur- und Geistesgeschichte," *Nachrichten der Akademie der Wissenschaften in Göttingen*, 1 (1949), 109-150.

14 J. C. Gottsched, *Ausführliche Redekunst* (5th ed. Leipzig, 1759), 122.

15 Mauritius Vogt, *Conclave Thesauri Magnae Artis Musicae* (Prague, 1719), 155-157.

16 John Dennis, The Advancement and Reformation of Modern Poetry (London, 1701), 32-33.

17 Dockhorn, "Die Rhetorik," 149.

18 Bond., Spectator, III, 516.

19 Ibid., I, 81.

20 Ibid., IV, 585.

21 Peter Smithers, The Life of Joseph Addison (Oxford: Clarendon Press, 1968), 468.

22 Johann Mattheson, Das neu-eröffnete Orchestre (Hamburg, 1713), 320: Kurtz von der eigentlichen Materie so wol der Music als Mahlerey zu reden, so ist bekandt, daß diese die Farbe, jene aber den Klang zu bearbeiten hat. Ob nun eins dem andern vorzusetzen, solches gebe denjenigen anheim, die den Unterschied zwischen Fühlen und Hören kennen, welches en jeder vernünfftiger und gesunder Mensch thun wird. Denn die Farbe die einer fühlen und sehen kan, ist eine blosse irdische Materie und hat ein gantz grobes Corpus; der Klang aber kan weder gesehen noch gefühlet, sondern allein gehöret werden und ist dannenhero so zu reden nichts materielles, sondern vielmehr gantz spirituelles, und proprie genommen, was unbegreifliches.

23 Alexander Malcolm, A Treatise of Musick, Speculative, Practical, and Historical (Edinburgh, 1721), 547.

24 Ibid., 597-598.

25 John Wilson, Roger North: Being a Selection of his Essays written between the years c.1695-1728 (London: Novello, 1959), 59.

26 Ibid., 92.

27 Ibid., 133-145.

28 Wit and Mirth: or, Pills to Purge Melancholy (London, 1719-1720), III, 10-15.

29 James Ralph, The Touchstone: or, Historical, Critical, Political, Philosophical, and Theological Essays on the reigning Diversions of the Town (London, 1728), 27.

30 The Poems of Henry Carey, ed. by Frederick T. Wood (London: Scholar's Press, 1930), 261; see Dennis R. Martin, The Operas and Operatic Style of John Frederick Lampe (Detroit: Detroit Monographs in Musicology, Number 8, 1985), 43-47; see also Ellen Harris, "An American Offers Advice to Handel," in American Choral Review, XXVI (1985), 55-62.

31 Ralph, Touchstone, 59.

32 Walter John Hipple, Jr., The Beautiful, The Sublime, and the Picturesque in Eighteenth-Century British Aesthetic Theory (Carbondale, Illinois: Southern Illinois University Press, 1957), ignores Ralph altogether.

33 Johann Mattheson, Das forschende Orchestre (Hamburg, 1721), 287.

34 Johann Mattheson, Critica musica (Hamburg, 1722-1725), I, 214n: Der Genius thut das Beste, das meiste, ja, fast alles bey der Sache; nicht die Kunst, welche weiter nichts als eine Handlangerinn abgibt.

35 Ibid., I, 248.

36 George Buelow, "Heinichen," in New Grove's Dictionary, 8, 439.

37 See Mattheson, Das neu-eröffnete Orchestre, 104; and Das beschützte Orchestre (Hamburg, 1717), 104.

38 Richard Tanner, Johann David Heinichen als dramatischer Komponist: Ein Beitrag zur Geschichte der Oper (Leipzig: Breitkopf & Härtel, 1916), 1, 1n-2n.

39 Johann David Heinichen, Der General-Baß in der Composition (Dresden, 1728), 34n-35n.

40 Ernst Gottlieb Baron, Untersuchung des Instruments der Lauten (Nuremberg, 1727), 152-153; trans. by Douglas Alton Smith (Redondo Beach, California: Instrumenta Antiqua, 1976), 152-153; 180: Ich habe desswegen hierher gesetzt, damit man sehen kan wie reich ein einziger Concentus sey viele andre Passagen zu gebähren. Kommt nun noch ein inventioses Ingenium darzu das ziemlich fundamental ist, so kan es nicht anders seyn, es müsse

durch so vieles Versetzen und Unkehren der Thöne, ein gutes und schönes Praeludium heraus kommen.

41 Ibid., 115; 137: Will man nun etwas erfinden, muss man mit einem guten Ingenio versehen seyn. Nun ist eine jede Erfindung an und vor sich selbst wie Gold in seinem Ertzte, welches allererst von seinen Schlacken muss gesäubert werden, hierzu muss nun das Jugement das meiste thun.

42 Ibid., 153; 181-182.

43 Ibid., 154; 183: Weil man nun leichtlich den Urgrund von solcher Meinung einsiehet, so thut man wohl, wenn man solche Leute, denen Gott besondere und extraordinaire Gaben gegeben, hochhalte, und so viel möglich, ihr Bestes befödere.

44 Ibid., 179; 216-217: Solche Leute haben schon gemeiniglich ihre Hölle auf der Welt, und fressen sich in ihren obscuren Winckeln das Leben selber ab.

45 John Frederick Lampe, <u>The Art of Musick</u> (London, 1740), 5.

46 Johann Adolph Scheibe, <u>Critischer Musicus</u> (Hamburg, 1738), 8, 57.

47 Ibid., 5, 33.

48 Ibid., 7, 51; see also Wilheim, "Scheibe," 92-93.

49 Ibid., 4, 26.

50 Ibid., 10, 75: Der Componist muss vornehmlich eine starke Einbildungskraft und dann ein vernünftiges Nachdenken besitzen.

51 Ibid., 65, 307: von Natur feurig und geistreich.

52 Ibid., 9, 66.

53 Scheibe, <u>Critischer Musicus</u> (2nd ed.; Hamburg, 1745), 8, 82-83.

54 Ibid., 8, 78n: Ich finde im sechsten Theile des englischen Zuschauers, und zwar auf der 96sten Seite der

deutschen Übersetzung eine merkwüdige Stelle, die allhier einen Platz verdienet. Addison handelt daselbst von der Belustigung der Einbildungskraft. Eine Materie, die von einem Componist wohl verdienet, nachgelesen zu werden, weil sie zu der Verbesserung seiner Erfindungen gehöret.

55 Addison, Spectator, III, 559. This is essay No. 416 from June of 1712.

56 Scheibe, Critischer Musicus, 2nd. ed., 8, 83n: Diese Gedanken sind der Musik sehr vortheilhaft, zumal sie den Unterschied sehr deutlich bemerken, der sich zwischen wahren und falschen Ausdrückungen befindet. Und gewiss, eine ausschweifende Einbildungskraft hat manchen frühzeitigen Componisten verleitet, auf Dinge zu verfallen, die nimmermehr auszudrücken sind; und die zugleich eben so lächerlich herauskommen, als wenn ein Maler die Verbindungsformeln einer Rede durch seine Bildnisse ausdrücken wollte.

57 Ibid., 55, 517n: man wird sie mit eben dem Vergnügen lesen, als ich sie selbst schon oft gelesen habe.

58 Lorenz Mizler, Die neu-erffnete musikalische Bibliothek (Leipzig, 1736-1754), II, iii, 1, 10n.

59 Ibid., I, v, 1, 28.

60 Ibid., I, v, 1, 28n.

61 Ibid., II, ii, 1, 227-232.

62 Johann Mattheson, Der vollkommene Capellmeister (Hamburg, 1738), 123; trans. by Ernest C. Harriss (Ann Arbor: UMI Research Press, 1981), 285: ob ich gleich selbst, meines Orts, keinen grossen Staat darauf mache.

63 Ibid., 132; 298-299.

64 Ibid., 132; 298-299: 1) Wenn man eines vortrefflichen Componisten Arbeit, zumahl dafern derselbe etwa einerley Materie mit der unsrigen behandlet hat, vorher wol ein- und ansiehet.
2) Wenn man sich eine Leidenschafft fest eindrückt, und sich gleichsam darin vertiefft, als wäre man in der That andächtig, verliebt, zornig, hönisch, betrübt, erfreuet, u.

s. w. dieses ist gewiss der sicherste Weg zu gantz unvermutheten Erfindungen.
3) Kan man auch in einer eintzigen Melodie verschiedene Erfindungen anbringen, und so zu reden fast augenblicklich, auf unerwartete Art, mit denselben abwechseln: welches die Zuhörer vergnüglich überraschet; wenn nur sonst dem Zusammenhange oder der Haupt-Absicht dadurch nicht zu nahe geschiehet.

65 Ibid., 12; 41: Also fällt es weg, daß die singende Musick eingentlich und ursprunglich älter seyn sollte denn die spielende: sintemahl auch den Engeln und Heiligen in der Bibel allerhand Instrumente, absonderlich Harfen und Posaunen, als besäitete und blasende Werckzeuge, begeleget werden, und sie gewisslich eben sowol gespielet, als gesungen haben, ehe denn Adam erschaffen worden.

66 Ibid., 11; 39. The excerpt form Paradise Lose is from book V. v. 144-151.

67 Mizler, Bibliothek, II, 1, 3, 40: Ein jeder vernünftiger siehet von selbsten, daß Gott und die gluckseligen Geister zu ihrer Glückseligkeit keine musicalische Instrumente nötig haben.

68 Ibid., II., i, 3, 40.

69 J. H. Tisch, "Milton and the German Mind in the Eighteenth Century," in Studies in the Eighteenth Century. Papers Presented at the David Nichol Smith Memorial Seminar (Canberra: Australian National University Press, 1968), 216.

70 Athanasius Kircher, Musurgia universalis (Rome, 1650), II, 364-367.

CHAPTER VIII

CONCLUSIONS

Although in the preceding chapters various aspects of early eighteenth-century musical thought in Britain and Germany have been explored, there can be no real sense of finality in our investigation. Some questions have been answered, but many remain. Connections have been shown, but others await discovery. Perhaps our frustration can be eased somewhat by the realization that finality may not be the best goal after all. The vacillations and inconsistencies found in the writings of eighteenth-century Germans and Britons indicate that the historian's goal may not be some "supreme destination," but the journey itself.

To facilitate this journey various routes have been travelled. First, a chronological approach to the material was taken. Second, personalities were presented and, when possible, interrelationships. Third, four important aesthetic issues were examined. Finally, all of this was done in a "two-nation" context, that is, as a part of an overall attempt to show the exchange of ideas between British and German musical thinkers. Though diffuse, this method served two important functions: to provide that a wide variety of material be examined, and to present eighteenth-century musical thought as closely as possible in the manner it was originally understood.

If we wish to speak of goals, perhaps the easiest to attain was the showing of relationships between British and German musical thought. Milton and Kircher (see Appendix I), Addison, Mattheson, and Scheibe, as well as the impact of philosophers like Locke and Shaftesbury in Germany, all provide ample evidence of the extent of this intercultural exchange. In the case of Malcolm, Pepusch, and Lampe, it was possible to show German influence in Britain. Even so, the former exchange, that flowing of ideas from Britain to Germany, must be seen as the more powerful. The tremendous influence of British philosophers--interpreted by Wolff--on German musical writers is a verifiable fact. The realm of literary theory provides similar examples. German musical writers, especially Mattheson and Scheibe, displayed an appreciation for British poets that preceded the pro-British (Miltonian) revolution that rocked the German literary world in the middle of the century.

On a more immediate level it has been possible to show strong personal relationships between writers, and even between nations. In Germany the amount of interaction was by far the more intense. Mattheson knew all his contemporaries, in most cases personally. In Britain no close contacts existed between persons like Lord North and James Ralph, and in general the level of interaction between British writers on music was slight. Pepusch's clumsy attacks on Lampe or Malclom hardly compare with Mizler's stinging comments to Mattheson, or Mattheson's sarcasm on Wolff's grammar. Whereas the most entertaining sources of criticism in Britain were the literary men like Addison and Dennis, most musical writers in Britain lived in isolation. Malcolm, for example, cited Shaftesbury, but he never integrated the philosopher's ideas into his own work. The opposite can be seen in Germany, where Mizler and Baron used Christian Wolff as their ticket to proper philosophical "weightiness." In Germany it was also possible to find writers who based their ideas directly on British philosophers. Mattheson's infatuation with Locke in Das forschende Orchestre will remain one of the outstanding examples of Anglomania in eighteenth-century Germany. While less spectacular, German influence made itself felt in Britain through men like Malcolm and North, but perhaps even more so through German immigrants like Pepusch, Lampe, and others.

There were indeed direct and, in some cases, personal contacts between British and German writers on music. There is no guesswork here. Germans consistently chose to support their arguments on certain matters by citing British writers. It is even possible to show the influence of Germans on British writers, though the results are not so spectacular. On the basis of these facts it seems logical that a strong case for the actual exchange of aesthetic ideas between the nations can be made. But caution must be our guide. Discussions of aesthetic trends, no matter what their merit may be, can mislead. A scheme of development may show why something occurred later on, but does not really tell the reader much about what was important to early eighteenth-century musicians.

There are two areas of aesthetic thought in which German musical writers were prophetic. By increasing their interest in British culture, writers like Mattheson and

Scheibe managed to voice the unconscious longing for an *independent* system of musical aesthetics. It is probable that this would have occurred in any case, but Milton's poetry and Addison's admiration for it made a profound impression on German-speaking intellectuals (notably the Swiss) and musical writers. Of course, our study has also shown that other writers were ambivalent or hostile to such ideas. Baron, for example, considered the imagination a rather dangerous aspect of the musician's psyche. Mizler was unrelenting in his distaste for the references to Milton in Mattheson's *Capellmeister*. Thus, prophetic or not, Mattheson's fascination with Milton no doubt seemed odd to most musicians in 1739. Indeed, if one were asked in 1740 who the greatest German writer on music was the response could just as easily have been Mizler as Mattheson.

The other "prophetic" trend in British and German musical thought was the decline of interest in both nations in the affections, in the concept of imitation, and taste. All three "systems" of thought were, by 1740, mentioned by musical writers more out of a sense of obligation than necessity. Nobody would have denied, for example, that music raised the passions, but there was plenty of opinion that music did *more*. The astonishing *Verwissenschaftlichung* of the affections in Germany by Heinichen and Mattheson must be seen as an aberration, not a barometer of musical thought at mid-century. Actually, by the 1730s British and German writers had essentially dropped the idea of the affections as it had been developed in the previous century. Instead, the concept was amended and adapted to fit new schemes. Thus when Mattheson says "the affections are everything" in his *Capellmeister* he was really saying "melody is everything." The early eighteenth-century musical writers had placed the concept of the affections on trial and found it wanting. By 1740 the idea that rhetorical concepts could actually be transmitted to musical models was considered doubtful.

Another term which showed a decline of popularity was taste. The concept had blown into the eighteenth century like a summer thunderstorm, leaving the musical writings of the early decades of the century so soaked with observations on _goût_ as to make them almost unreadable. Writers like Mattheson and Ralph revelled in the freedom which the term allowed, and the concept of an inborn judgement must have seemed attractive to many intellectuals in Germany and Britain. It provided, if nothing else, a convenient explanation for musical talent. Still, by the 1730s the storm was passing, and most writers already had found shelter under the more substantial tenets of empiricism. The all-inclusiveness of the concept of taste proved to be its downfall. Even Mattheson, whose _Das neu-eröffnete Orchestre_ was one enormous glorification of "taste," became suspicious of the term by the next decade. His confidence in finding "rules of taste" in the 1720s dissolved in the 1730s. Scheibe's attempt to draw distinctions between taste and style, laudable though they may have been, were attacked by Mattheson and Mizler. While the study of taste continued to fascinate a wide range of intellectuals in mid- and even late-eighteenth-century Europe, musical writers in Germany and Britain had discarded the concept by the end of the early Enlightenment.

The final aesthetic casualty of the early eighteenth-century was the concept of imitation. As in the case of all giants, the downfall of this ancient juggernaut was thunderous indeed. The liberation of musical thought from the restrictive precepts of seventeenth-century literary doctrine was one of the central accomplishments of musical thinkers in the era of the Enlightenment. One cannot argue with Anna Tumarkin's choice of words: there was indeed an Überwindung of the concept of mimesis. The argument begins, however, when we attempt to decide just when this "conquest" occurred. This study has shown that the date must be placed in the 1720s: both Ralph and Mattheson departed radically from the view that music was an imitative art. Serauky and Goldschmidt were wrong in choosing the Lübeck Capellmeister Caspar Ruetz as the writer responsible for upsetting the theory of imitation in music in 1754.[1] Another aspect of this break-away from the doctrine of imitation can be seen in Scheibe's conflict with J. S. Bach. For Scheibe and others, naturalness in music meant simplicity. The old concept of mimesis, with its academic rules, did not fit into the new aesthetic of the 1730s. In its place Scheibe substituted a doctrine of naturalness which did not depend on rules but on spontaneity and grace. Though his arguments were different, Scheibe was also voicing his rejection of the old doctrine of imitation.

With the fall of ancient aesthetic theories the eighteenth-century musical writer was left to discover new aesthetic venues. In Germany a whole world of musical journalism sprang into existence. Marpurg, Kirnberger, C. P. E. Bach, Quantz, Leopold Mozart, and many other musicians became well-known writers. Even Britain could boast of Charles Avison and Dr. Burney by the end of the century. Throughout Europe the liberation of musical thought from archaic systems contributed to a rethinking of the place of music in schemes of the arts. By 1800 music had ceased to be the poor sister to poetry. By 1900 it was the art to which all others seemed to aspire.

Thus the musical thought of the early eighteenth century contained the seeds of much of what was to come. Even so, it might be better to think more in terms of continuity than genesis. The desire to place an enormous caesura mark over the year 1750, to delineate the high baroque from the classical style (tempting as it was to nineteenth-century German musicologists) cannot be justified. The year of J. S. Bach's death did not mark the end of an era--his era had ended long before. Hugo Riemann's decision to place the _neue Keime_ of the new style in the 1740s, a decision followed by many twentieth-century historians, was incorrect.[2] Writers on musical thought had begun to undermine the aesthetic basis of the baroque early in the eighteenth century. Indeed, the transisiton from baroque to classical took place over a long period of time, facilitated by the writings of numerous figures who, at least until recently, have been greatly neglected.

Yet this transition remains shrouded in mystery. A considerable amount of information about early eighteenth-century musical thought in Germany and Britain remains to be collected: Mattheson's fascination for Locke needs to be explored further; Shaftesbury's impact on German musical writers should be investigated; more evidence of German influence on British musical thought can certainly be found. Even greater is the need for a more balanced study of the Enlightenment in music, where French influences are examined alongside those of Britain, Germany, and Italy. Similarly, little work has been done which attempts to place musical thought into a philosophical perspective. Important literary movements should be taken into account, and a broader, interdisciplinary approach needs to be taken. For the eighteenth-century musician, music was an art which was not limited by specializations or nationalities. Nor was it unusual to find musical writers who were active not in one career, but several. For the modern scholar to understand such men is a challenge. We must overcome our own historical and personal limitations if we are ever to understand the intensity and beautiful variety of eighteenth-century musical thought.

1 Hugo Goldschmidt, Die Musikästhetik des 18. Jahrhunderts (Zurich and Leipzig: Rascher, 1915), 139; Walter Serauky, Die musikalische Nachahmungsästhetik im Zeitraum von 1700 bis 1850 (Münster: Helios, 1929), 77.

2 Hugo Riemann, Handbuch der Musikgeschichte: Zweiter Band, Dritter Teil: Die Musik des 18. und 19. Jahrhunderts, 2nd ed., (Leipzig: Breitkopf & Härtel, 1922), 119-124.

APPENDIX I

Kircher and Milton: A German-British Exchange of Musical Thought

There are numerous references to music in the works of John Milton, perhaps the best known being found in his Paradise Lost, written between 1658 and 1665. In this excerpt Milton describes the music of the angels:

> Speak, ye who best can tell, ye Sons of Light,
> Angels--for ye behold him, and with songs
> And choral symphonies, day without night,
> Circle his throne rejoicing--ye in Heaven;
> On earth join all ye creatures, to extol
> Him first, him last, him midst, and without end.
>
> Paradise Lost 5.160-165

And similarly:

> Nor with less dread the loud
> Ethereal trumpet from on high began to blow;
> At which command the powers militant,
> That stood for Heaven, in mighty quadrate joined
> Of union irresistible move on
> In silence their bright legions, to the sound
> Of instrumental harmony, that breathed
> Heroic ardor to adventurous deeds
> Under their god-like leaders, in the cause

Of God and his Messiah.
Paradise Lost 6.59-68

Instruments, especially the organ, are often mentioned:

The harp had work and rested not, the solemn pipe
And dulcimer, all organs of sweet stop,
All sounds on fret by string or golden wire,
Tempered soft tunings, intermixed with voice
Choral or unison.
Paradise Lost 7.594-599

As are images of organ playing:

He looked, and saw a spacious plain, whereon
Were tents of various hue; by some were herds
Of cattle grazing; others whence the sound
Of instruments that made melodious chime
Was heard, of harp and organ; and who moved
Their stops and chords was seen; his volant touch
Instinct, through all proportions low and high
Fled and pursued transverse the resonant fugue.
Paradise Lost 11.556-563

It is easy enough to account for Milton's knowledge of, and interest in, music and musical instruments, particularly the organ. John Milton the elder was a composer of some distinction, though his career as a scrivener occupied much of his time.[1] We know that in 1632, when the Milton family moved to Horton in Buckinghamshire, the elder Milton brought his portative organ and other instruments with him.[2] The poet was taught by his father to sing and to play keyboard instruments.[3] Milton reports his musical activities in his Defenso Secunda of 1654 (8.120-121):

At my father's rural dwelling, to which he had retired to live out his remaining days, being at my ease, I devoted myself entirely to reading the Greek and Latin writers; sometimes, however, I changed from the country

> to the city, either for the purchase of books, or to learn something new about Mathematics or Music, which at that time were my principal delight. 4

The description of the angelic choirs, and the references to the organ are cited by Sigmund Spaeth in his work Milton's Knowledge of Music, first published in 1913. Spaeth makes several observations about Milton's references to music, among them that Athanasius Kircher's Musurgia universalis "contains some strikingly Miltonic ideas."[5] Actually, if there is a connection between the two men the reverse seems likely. Could such a connection exist, and if so, how could Kircher's work influence Milton's?

At the outset it must be pointed out that Milton's interest in music involved more than singing and playing. During his Cambridge years (between 1625 and 1629) he wrote an essay entitled De Sphaerum Concentu which took ideas from Plato and Pythagoras. He even voiced his own opinion as to why we no longer are able to hear this special type of music:

> The reason why we are unable to hear this harmony is the foolhardy theft of Prometheus, which, among so many ills that it brought to mankind, robbed us of this faculty of hearing. Nor shall we be allowed to enjoy this faculty again, so long as we are overwhelmed by sin and grow brutish with beastly desires. But if our hearts should grow to a snowy purity, then our ears would be filled and ring with the most sweet Music of the revolving stars. 6

Obviously, Milton was aware of speculative musical thought even before he travelled to Italy on a trip which began in April of 1638 and ended with his return to Britain in August of 1639. During his travels Milton crossed

France, stopped off in Switzerland, and spent several months in Italy. Milton wrote the following brief description of his journey, also found in the Defenso Secunda:

> Taking ship at Nice, I arrived at Genoa and afterwards visited Leghorn, Pisa, and Florence. In the latter city, which I have always more particularly esteemed for the elegance of its dialect, its genius, and its taste, I stopped about two months: when I contracted an intimacy with many persons of rank and learning; and was a constant attendant at their literary parties; a practice which prevails there, and tends so much to the diffusion of knowledge, and the preservation of friendship. No time will ever abolish the agreeable recollections which I cherish of Jaco Baddi, Carolo Dati, Frescobaldo, Cultellero, Bonomatthai, Clementillo, Francisco, and many others. From Florence I went to Sienna, thence to Rome, where, after I had spent about two months in viewing the antiquities of that renowned city, where I experienced the most friendly attentions form Lucas Holstein, and other learned and ingenious men, I continued my route to Naples. There I was introduced by a certain recluse, with whom I had travelled from Rome, to John Baptista Manso, marquis of Villa, a nobleman of distinguished rank and authority. 7

There is another document from Milton's trip which is of interest to us, a letter to Lucas Holstein from Florence, written after Milton's visit to Rome:

> When I went up to the Vatican for the purpose of meeting you, you received me, a total stranger to you (unless perchance anything had been previously said about me to you by Alexander Cherubini) with the utmost courtesy. Immediately admitted with politeness into the Museum, I was allowed to behold both the manuscript Greek authors set forth with our explanations....then I could not but believe that it was in consequence of the mention you made to me to the most excellent Cardinal Francesco Barberini, that, when he, a few days after, gave that public musical entertainment with truly Roman magnificence, he himself, waiting at the doors and

> seeking me out in so great a crowd, nay, almost laying hold of me by the hand, admitted me with a truly most honorable manner. 8

What conclusions can we draw from these two documents? The most striking fact they reveal is that Milton came to know the music-loving Cardinal Francesco Barberini. This is not so unexpected, however, since Barberini was "by self-appointment" patron of England and Scotland and famed as an entertainer of British guests to Rome.[9] It was also natural to assume that Barberini had been told of Milton's arrival by Lucas Holstein, since Holstein (or more correctly, Holste) was one of the Cardinal's secretaries and curator of Barberini's personal library.[10]

After Milton's sojourn in Rome (including a short trip to Naples and back) he returned to Florence. It was during this visit that Milton attended a meeting of the _Svogliate_, a literary circle, and read some of his own Latin poems. It seems probable that Milton read the three he had written in praise of Leonora Baroni, the famous Mantuan singer whom Milton had heard in Rome.[11] Interestingly enough, as Spaeth has pointed out, in attendance at this same meeting was none other than Giovanni Battista Doni, influential poet and writer on music, most notably in his _Compendio del trattato_ (Rome, 1635). During the meeting Doni also read (we are not sure what) and it seems safe to assume that Milton and Doni must have met at this time.

Does Milton's acquaintance with Holste, Barberini, or Doni give us any reason to suspect that the poet might have known Athanasius Kircher? Kircher was, after all, living in Rome at this time and had been there for five years. This fact provides the most obvious clue to a connection between Kircher and Milton, for it was by Cardinal

Francesco Barberini's wish that the General of the Jesuit order, Mutius Vitlelleschi, made Kircher professor of mathematics, physics, and oriental languages at the Collegio Romano in 1633.[12] Kircher had planned to accept a post as court mathematician in Vienna, but, upon arriving in Rome and hearing news of his appointment, never left the papal city again for any length of time. The longest trip he took was during 1637, when he served as personal confessor to the Landgraf Friedrich von Hessen-Darmstadt on a trip to Malta, an episode to which we shall return. With the constant aid of Cardinal Barberini, Kircher moved in the highest circles in Rome and was a welcome guest in many of the best households.[13]

Just as Barberini served as patron to Kircher, so did he also favor Giovanni Battista Doni.[14] Thus Kircher and Doni had the same patron, and they were good friends. Doni dedicated one of his discourses to Kircher (his _Del sintono di Didimo e di Tolomeo_).[15] Kircher cites Doni in his works as well, including the _Musurgia universalis_.[16] It is on this evidence that Spaeth based his supposition. Because Milton knew both Doni and Barberini and was in Rome during the same time period as Kircher, Milton might have seen parts of Kircher's _Musurgia_, which was then in progress. Spaeth also supported this argument by poining out the similarities between discussions of music by the two men, though he does not qualify his statement. Robert H. West, writing some forty years later, makes the same suggestion in _Milton and the Angels_, but he does not seem to have known Spaeth's work.[17] West was struck by Milton's discussions of heavenly music and also pointed out the influence of Robert Flud on the poet. Several other scholars, notably Denis Saurat, have noted similarities between the writings of Flud, Kircher, and Milton.[18] Saurat links the three in their knowledge of the Zohar, an account of non-orthodox Jewish traditions gathered together in thirteenth-century Spain and published in Italy in the sixteenth century.[19] I am inclined to agree with Harris Francis Fletcher, who found Saurat's parallels interesting but far from conclusive in his work on the subject.[20] Even so, West felt that these parallels were strong enough evidence that the men knew one another, and on West's authority J. C. Boswell included Kircher's Oedipus Aegyptiacus in his reconstruction of Milton's library.[21] Milton knew Kircher's work, and perhaps even Kircher, but the most conclusive evidence for this lies one step beyond Spaeth's argument and involves the third member of the Barberini-Doni-Holste triangle.

Lukas Holste, or Holstein as Milton called him, was born in 1595 and educated at the Akademisches Gymnasium in Rostock.[22] Joachim Burmeister, the author of Musica poetica, taught there during this period as well. Holste later studied in Leiden and eventually travelled in the company of the brothers Otto and Nikolaus von Qualen to London, where he stayed for two years. He then accompanied the von Qualens to Paris where, in 1624, he was converted to the Catholic faith by the Jesuit Jacques Sirmond. Holste met Francesco Barberini in Paris, and the Cardinal took him back to Rome with him to work in the family library and later in the Vatican.

The relationship between Kircher and Holste becomes certain when one discovers that Holste, famous as a proselytizer of the Catholic faith, listed none other than the Landgraf Friedrich von Hessen-Darmstadt as one of his converts, the same aristocrat whom Kircher served as personal confessor during the former's trip to Malta in 1637. Kircher and Holste accompanied the future Cardinal on this journey, and there can be no doubt the two knew one another well.

On the basis of this evidence it would seem unlikely that Milton could have known Holste, Doni, and Barberini without meeting Athanasius Kircher. Milton's previous interest in speculative music, as well as the parallels in his works and the writings of Flud and Kircher, support the possibility for such a meeting. The influence of the German upon Milton has been alluded to by writers, even though they had little knowledge of the two men's biographies. Milton's probable knowledge of Kircher and his work, and the poet's importance for later writers like Mattheson, make Milton a surprisingly important figure in British and German musical thought for several generations after his death.

1 See Ernest Brennecke, Jr., John Milton the Elder and His Music (New York, 1938).

2 Ibid., 121.

3 Ibid., 136.

4 See Harris Francis Fletcher, The Intellectual Development of John Milton (Urbana, Illinois: University of Illinois Press, 1961), 351.

5 Sigmund Spaeth, Milton's Knowledge of Music (Princeton: University Library Press, 1913), 23.

6 E. M. M. Tillyard, Milton (New York: Dial, 1930), 375.

7 James Holly Hanford, A Milton Handbook (New York: F. S. Crofts, 1933), 25-26.

8 John Arthos, Milton and the Italian Cities (New York: Barnes & Noble, 1968), 53-54.

9 David Masson, The Life of John Milton (London: Macmillan, 1875), I, 632.

10 Ibid., I, 631.

11 Arthos, Milton, 55.

12 Ulf Scharlau, Athanasius Kircher (1601-1680) als Musikschriftsteller (Marburg: n.p., 1969), 14.

13 Ibid., 16.

14 Claude V. Palisca, "Doni," in New Grove's Dictionary, 5, 550.

15 See Due Trattati di Gio. Battista Doni, in Barberina amphichordos: accedunt eiusdum opera (Florence, 1763), 349-355.

16 Works cited by Kircher include the Compendio de Trattato (Rome, 1635), and the Lyra Barberina (Florence, 1763), 349-355.

17 Robert H. West, Milton and the Angles (Athens, Georgia: University of Georgia Press, 1955), 159.

18 Denis Saurat, Milton: Man and Thinker (New York: Dial, 1925).

19 Saurat, Milton, 281.

20 Harris Francis Fletcher, Milton's Rabbinical Readings (Urbana, Illinois: University of Illinois Press, 1930), 7.

21 Jackson Campbell Boswell, Milton's Library: A Catalogue of the Remains of John Milton's Library and an Annotated Reconstruction of Milton's Library and Ancillary Readings (New York: Garland, 1975), 150. Boswell includes eight of Flud's works, including the Utrisque cosmi.

22 See Peter Fuchs, "Holste," in Neue Deutsche Biographie (Berlin: Duncker & Humblot, 1971), 9, 548-550.

APPENDIX II

John Locke and Johann Mattheson

The influence of John Locke upon Johann Mattheson is itself a topic worthy of an entire study. Here I will only list Mattheson's references--most of them previously unnoticed--to the philosopher's Of Human Understanding in Das forschende Orchestre.

1. Page 32-33: paragraph 6 and 7. Refers to Locke, I. ii. 15.
2. Page 65n: Refers to Locke, II, xviii, 3. Mattheson reproduces the entire paragraph in English.
3. Page 83-83n: paragraph 58. Refers to Locke II. i. 2. and II. vii. 10.
4. Page 111-112n: paragraph 93. Refers to Locke, I. ii. 1. and I. ii. 5.
5. Page 112-113: paragraph 94. Refers to above passage.
6. Page 116-117n: paragraph 97. Refers to Locke, I. i. 5.

7. Page 120-121n: paragraph 101. Refers to II. i. 4. Mattheson includes his translation into German as well as Locke's original text.

8. Page 125-126n: paragraph 110. Refers to Locke, II. i. 4. Locke's conception of the operations of the mind (die Wirkungen des Verstandes) is presented by Mattheson.

9. Page 139-140: paragraph 5. Refers to Locke, I. ii. 9.

10. Page 148: paragraph 12. Refers to Locke, II. xi. 6.

BIBLIOGRAPHY: PRIMARY SOURCES

Addison, Joseph, and Richard Steele, The Tatler. Ed. by George A. Aitken, New York: Hadley and Matthews, 1899.

__________, The Spectator. Ed. by Donald R. Bond, Oxford: Clarendon Press, 1965.

Baron, Ernst Gottlieb, Historisch-theoretisch und practische Untersuchung des Instruments der Lauten Nuremberg, 1727.

Baumgarten, Alexander Gottlieb, Meditationes Philosophicae De Nonnullis Ad Poema Pertinentibus. Trans. by Karl Aschenbrenner and William B. Holther, Los Angeles: University of California Press, 1954.

Bedford, Arthur. The Great Abuse of Music. London: 1711.

Bodmer, J. J., and J. J. Breitinger, Critische Briefe. Zurich, 1749.

__________, Die Discourse der Mahlern. Zurich, 1721.

Bodmer, J. J., Critische Abhandlung von dem Wunderbaren in der Poesie. Zurich, 1740.

Brounker, Lord. Musicae Compendium. London, 1653.

Butler, Charles. The Principles of Musick. London, 1636.

Cooper, Anthony Ashley, 3rd Earl of Shaftesbury. Characteristicks of Men, Manners, Opinions, Times. Fifth edition, revised. London, 1732.

Dennis, John. The Critical Works of John Dennis. Ed. by Edward Niles Hooker. Baltimore: Johns Hopkins Press, 1939.

Dodwell, Henry. A Treatise Concerning the Lawfulness of Instrumental Musick in the Holy Offices. London, 1700.

Doppelmayr, Johann Gabriel. Historische Nachricht von den nürnbergerischen Mathematicis und Künstlern. Nuremberg, 1730.

Dubos, Jean-Baptiste. Critical Reflections on Poetry, Painting, and Music. Trans. Trans. by Thomas Nugent. London, 1748.

Gottsched, Johann Christoph. Versuch einer critischen Dichtkunst. Ed. by Joachim Birke, Johann Christoph Gottsched: Ausgewählte Werke., Vol. VI. Berlin: de Gruyter, 1973.

___________. Die vernünftigen Tadlerinnen. Leipzig, 1748.

___________. Handlexikon, oder Kurzgefaßtes Wörterbuch der schönen Wissenschaften und freyen Künste. Leipzig, 1760.

Gottsched, Louise Adelgunde. Briefe, die Einführung des englischen Geschmacks in Schauspielen. Leipzig, 1760.

Grassineau, James. A Musical Dictionary. London, 1740.

Heinichen, Johann David. Neu-erfundene und gründliche Anweisung...zu vollkommener Erlernung des General-Baßes. Hamburg, 1711.

___________. Der General-Baß in der Composition. Dresden, 1728.

Holder, William. A Treatise of the Natural Grounds and Principles of Harmony. London, 1731.

Home, Henry, Lord Kames. Elements of Criticism. Sixth edition. Edinburgh, 1775.

Hunold, Christian. Die allerneueste Art zur reinen und galanten Poesie zu gelangen. Hamburg, 1707.

Hutcheson, Francis. An Essay on the Nature and Conduct of the Passions and Affections with Illustrations on the Moral Sense. London, 1742.

___________. An Inquiry into the Original of our Ideas of Beauty and Virtue. Fourth edition. London, 1738.

Jackson, William. Priliminary Discourse to a Scheme, Demonstrating and Shewing the Perfection and Harmony of Sounds. London, 1726.

Keller, G. A Compleat Method for Attaining to Play a Thorough Bass upon either Organ, Harpsichord or Theorbo. London, 1715.

Krause, C. G. Von der musikalischen Poesie. Berlin, 1753.

Locke, John. Some Thoughts Concerning Education. Ninth edition. London, 1732.

__________. An Essay Concerning Human Understanding. London, 1692.

Malcolm, Alexander. A Treatise of Musick, Speculative, Practical, and Historical. Edinburgh, 1721.

Mattheson, Johann. Das neu-eröffnete Orchestre. Hamburg, 1713.

__________. Das beschützte Orchestre. Hamburg, 1717.

__________. Das forschende Orchestre. Hamburg, 1721.

__________. Critica Musica. Hamburg, 1722-1725.

__________. Der neu Göttingische, aber viel schlechter als die alten Lacedämonischen, urtheilende Ephorus. Hamburg, 1727.

__________. Der musicalische Patriot. Hamburg, 1728.

__________. Große General-Baß Schule. Hamburg, 1731.

__________. Kern melodischer Wissenschaft. Hamburg, 1737.

__________. Der vollkommene Capellmeister. Hamburg, 1739.

Mizler, Lorenz. Musikalischer Staarstecher. Leipzig, 1739-1740.

__________. Musikalische Bibliothek. Leipzig, 1736-1754.

__________. Anfangs-Gründe des General-Baßes. Leipzig, 1739.

Murschhauser, Francisum Xaverium. Academia Musico-Poetica Biparta. Nuremberg, 1721.

Nicolai, Ernst Anton. Die Verbindung der Musik mit der Artzneygelehrheit. Halle, 1745.

North, Roger. The Musicall Grammarian. Ed. by Sir Richard Terry. London: Oxford University Press, 1925.

__________. Memoirs of Musick. Ed. by Edward F. Rimbault. London: G. Bell, 1846.

__________. Roger North: Being an Selection of his Essays written during the years c.1695-1728. Ed. by John Wilson. London: Novello, 1959.

Pepusch, Johann Christoph. A Treatise on Harmony. London, 1731.

Prelleur, Peter. A Brief History of Musick. London, 1731.

Ralph, James. The Touchstone: or, Historical, Critical, Political, Philosophical, and Theological Essays on the reigning Diversions of the Town. London, 1728.

Rollin, Charles. The Method of Teaching and Studying the Belles Lettres, or an Introduction to Languages, Poetry, Rhetoric, History, Moral Philosophy, Physicks, & etc. With Reflections on Taste. London, 1737.

Scheibe, Johann Adolph. Compendium musices theoretico-practicum. Leipzig, 1736.

__________. Der critische Musicus. Second edition. Hamburg, 1745.

__________. Eine Abhandlung von den musicalischen Intervallen und Geschlechten. Hamburg, 1739.

__________. Abhandlung vom Ursprunge und Alter der Musik. Altona and Flensburg, 1754.

Scheibel, Gottfried Ephraim. Zufällige Gedancken von der Kirchen-Music. Frankfurt and Leipzig, 1721.

Stößel, Johann Christoph, and Johann David Stößel. Kurtzgefaßtes musicalisches Lexikon. Chemnitz, 1749.

Simpson, Christopher. A Compendium, or Introduction to Practical Musick. London, 1667.

Vockerodt, Gottfried. Mißbrauch der freyen Künste. Frankfurt, 1697.

Walter, Johann Gottfried. Musicalisches Lexikon, oder musicalische Bibliothec. Leipzig, 1732.

Wolff, Christian. Preliminary Discourse on Philosophy in General. Trans. by Richard J. Blackwell. Indianapolis and New York: Bobbs-Merrill, 1963.

BIBLIOGRAPHY: SECONDARY SOURCES

Abert, Hermann. Die Lehre vom Ethos in der griechischenMusik. (Sammlung musikwissenschaftlicher Arbeiten von deutschen Hochschulen, 2.) Leipzig: Breitkopf und Härtel, 1899.

Agar, Herbert. Milton and Plato. Princeton: Princeton University Press, 1928.

Aitken, George A. The Life of Richard Steele. London: William Isbister, 1889.

Alewyn, Richard. Johann Beer, Sein Leben, Von Ihm Selbst Erzählt. Ed. by Adolf Schmiedecke. Göttingen: Vandenhoeck & Ruprecht, 1965.

Allen, Don Cameron. The Harmonious Vision: Studies in Milton's Poetry. Baltimore: Johns Hopkins Press, 1954.

Arthos, John. Milton and the Italian Cities. New York: Barnes and Noble, 1968.

Ashbee, Andrew. "Robert Flud," in New Grove's Dictionary, Vol. 6, 633.

Atcherson, W. T. "Seventeenth-Century Music Theory: England," Journal of Music Theory, 16 (1972), 6-15.

Atkins, J. W. H. English Literary Criticism: 17th and 18th Centuries. New York: Barnes & Noble, 1950.

Auerbach, Erich. Mimesis: The Representation of Reality in Western Literature. Trans. by Willard Trask. Garden City, New York: Doubleday Books, 1953.

Baker, David and Jennifer. "A 17th-Century Dial Song," Musical Times, CXIX (1978), 590-593.

Bates, Walter J. From Classic to Romantic. New York: Harper & Brothers, 1946.

Baeumler, Alfred. Das Irrationalitätsproblem in der Ästhetik und Logik des 18. Jahrhunderts bis zur Kritik der Urteilskraft. Halle, 1923.

Beardsley, Monroe C. Aesthetics from Classical Greece to the Present. New York: MacMillan Company, 1966.

Beck, Lewis White. Early German Philosophy: Kant and his Predecessors. Cambridge, Mass.: The Belknap Press of Harvard Universtiy Press, 1969.

Becker, Heinz. "Die frühe Hamburgische Tagespresse als musikgeschichtliche Quelle," in Beiträge zur Hamburgischen Musikgeschichte. Ed. by Heinrich Husmann. Hamburg: University of Hamburg, 1956. (22-45.)

Benary, Peter. Die deutsche Kompositionslehre des 18. Jahrhunderts. Leipzig: Breitkopf & Härtel, 1961.

Bender, Wolfgang. J. J. Breitinger und J. J. Bodmer. Stuttgart: J. B. Metzler, 1973.

Bergmann, Ernst. Die Begründung der deutschen Ästhetik durch Alexander Gottlieb Baumgarten und Georg Friedrich Meier. Leipzig: Röder und Schunke, 1911.

Bernstein, John Andrew. Shaftesbury, Rousseau, Kant. London: Associated University Press, 1980.

Betz, Siegmund. "The Operatic Criticism of the Tatler and Spectator," Musical Quarterly, 31 (1945), 318-330.

Bimberg, Siegfried, ed. Handbuch der Musikästhetik. Leipzig: Deutscher Verlag für Musik, 1979.

Bing, Susi. Die Naturnachahmungstheorie bei Gottsched und den Schweizern und ihre Beziehung zu der

Dichtungstheorie der Zeit. Würzburg: Conrad Triltsch, 1934.

Birke, Joachim. Christian Wolffs Metaphysik und die Zeitgenössiche Literatur- und Musiktheorie: Gottsched, Scheibe, Mizler. Berlin: de Gruyter, 1966.

Blom, Eric. Music in England. New York: Penguin, 1947.

Bond, R. P. The Tatler: the Making of a Literary Journal. Cambridge: Cambridge University Press, 1971.

Bormann, Alexander von. Vom Laienurteil zum Kunstgefühl. Tübingen, 1974,

Bosker, A. Literary Criticism in the Age of Johnson. Groningen: J. B. Wolters, 1930.

Boswell, Jackson Campbell. Milton's Library: A Catalogue of the Remains of John Milton's Library in an Annotated Reconstruction of Milton's Library and Ancillary Readings. New York and London: Garland Publishing, 1975.

Brennecke, Ernest, Jr., John Milton the Elder and his Music. New York, 1938.

Brett, R. L. The Third Earl of Shaftesbury: A Study in Eighteenth-Century Literary Theory. London: Hutchinson's University Library, 1951.

Bridge, Frederick. "A 17th-Century View of Musical Education," Proceedings of the Royal Musical Association, XXVII (1901), 121-130.

Brockpähler, Renate. Handbuch zur Geschichte der Barockoper in Deutschland. Emsdetten: Verlag Lechte, 1970.

Brüggemann, Fritz. Gottscheds Lebens- und Kunstreform in den zwanziger und dreißiger Jahren. Leipzig: Reclam, 1935.

Bruford, Walter H. Germany in the eighteenth Century: the Social Background of the Literary Revival. London: Cambridge University Press, 1935.

Brunschwig, Henri. Enlightenment and Romanticism in Eighteenth-Century Prussia. Trans. by Frank Jellinek. Chicago: University of Chicago Press, 1974.

Buelow, George. "Heinichen," in New Grove's Dictionary, 8, 439.

____________. "Johann David Heinichen's Der Generalbaß in der Composition: a Critical Study with Annotated Translation of Selected Chapters." Ph.D. dissertation, University of Michigan, 1961. (Microfilm. Ann Arbor: University Microfilms.)

____________. "In Defence of J. A. Scheibe against J. S.. Bach," in Proceedings of the Royal Music Association, CI (1974-1975), 85-100.

____________. "The Loci Topici and Affect in Late Baroque Music: Heinichen's Practical Demonstration," Music Review, XXVIII (1966), 161-176.

____________. "Johann Mattheson and the invention of the Affektenlehre," in New Mattheson Studies, ed. by George Buelow and Hans Joachim Marx, Cambridge: Cambridge University Press, 1983, 393-407.

____________. "Mattheson," in New Grove's Dictionary, 11, 832-836.

____________. "Mizler," in New Grove's Dictionary, 12, 372-373.

____________. "Musical Rhetoric," in New Grove's Dictionary, 15, 801.

____________. "Music, Rhetoric, and the Concept of the Affections: A Selective Bibliography," Notes, XXX (1973-1974), 250-259.

____________. "Printz," in New Grove's Dictionary, 15, 275.

____________. "Ruetz," in New Grove's Dictionary, 16, 317-318.

____________. "Scheibe," in New Grove's Dictionary, 16, 599-601.

__________. "Seventeenth-Century Music Theory: Germany," Journal of Music Theory, 16 (1972), 36-49.

__________. Thorough-Bass Accompaniment According to Johann David Heinichen. Berkeley: University of California Press, 1966.

Burton, M. C. "Mr. Prendcourt and Roger North on Teaching Music," Musical Quarterly, XLIV (1958), 32-39.

Butcher, S. H. Aristotle's Theory of Poetry and Fine Art. Fourth edition. New York: Dover, 1951.

Butt, John. The Mid-Eighteenth Century. Oxford, 1980.

Cannon, Beekman C. Johann Mattheson, Spectator in Music. New Haven: Yale University Press, 1947.

Caspar, Max. Kopernikus und Kepler. Munich, 1948.

Cassirer, Ernst. "English Aesthetics," in Philosophy of the Enlightenment. Trans. by F. C. A. Koelln and J. P. Pettegrave.Boston: Beacon Press, 1965.

Cassirer, Ernst. The Philosophy of the Enlightenment. Princeton: Princeton University Press, 1951.

__________. Die Platonische Renaissance in England und die Schule von Cambridge. Leipzig: Teubner,1932.

Cauchy, V. "Epicureanism," in The New Catholic Encyclopedia. New York: McGraw-Hill, 1967. (Vol. V, 466-468.)

Chambers, Frank. Cycles of Taste. Cambridge, Mass.: Harvard Unversity Press, 1928.

__________. The History of Taste. New York: Columbia, 1932.

Chenette, L. F. "Music Theory in the British Isles During the Enlightenment." Unpubl. Ph.D. dissertation. Ohio State University, 1967.

Clark, A. F. B. Boileau and the French Classical Critics in England (1660-1830). Paris: Libraire Ancienne Edouard Champion, 1925.

Cowart, Georgia. _The Origins of Modern Musical Criticism: French and Italian Music 1600-1750_. Ann Arbor: UMI Research Press, 1981.

Cragg, G. R. _From Puritanism to the Age of Reason. A Study of Changes in Religious Thought within the Church of England 1660 to 1700_. Cambridge: Cambridge Universtiy Press, 1950.

Crüger, Johannes. _Joh. Christoph Gottsched und die Schweizer J. J. Bodmer und J. J. Breitinger_. Berlin and Stuttgart: W. Spemann, n. d.

Dahlhaus, Carl. _Musikästhetik_. Cologne: Hans Gerig, 1967; Trans. by William W. Austin, Cambridge: Cambridge University Press, 1982.

Damann, Rolf. "Werckmeister," in _MGG_, Vol. 16, 476-480.

__________. "Zur Musiklehre des Andreas Werckmeister," _Archiv für Musikwissenschaft_, 11 (1954).

Darenberg, Karl-Heinz. _Studien zur englischen Musikaesthetic des 18. Jahrhunderts._. Hamburg: Cram-de Gruyter, 1960.

David, Hans T., and Arthur Mendel. _The Bach Reader_. Second edition, revised. New York: Norton, 1966.

Davis, G. N. _German Thought and Culture in England, 1700-1770_. Chapel Hill: University Of North Carolina Press, 1955.

Dent, Edward J. _Foundations of English Opera_. Cambridge: Oxford University Press, 1928.

Dobree, Bonamy. _English Literature in the Early Eighteenth Century, 1700-1740_. Oxford: Clarendon Press, 1959.

Dockhorn, Klaus. _Deutscher Geist und angelsächsische Geistesgeschichte: Ein Versuch der Deutung ihres Verhältnisses_. Göttingen, Frankfurt, and Berlin: Musterschmidt Wissenschaftlicher Verlag, 1954.

__________. "Die Rhetorik als Quelle des vorromantischen Irrationalismus in der Literatur- und

Geistesgeschichte," in *Nachrichten der Akademie der Wissenschaften in Göttingen*, (1949), 109-150.

Draper, John W. *Eighteenth-Century English Aesthetics*. Heidelberg: n.p., 1931.

Elledge, Scott, editor. *Eighteenth-Century Critical Essays*. Ithaca: Cornell University Press, 1964.

Elliot, Kenneth, and Frederick Rimmer. *A History of Scottish Music*. London: British Broadcasting Corporation, 1973.

Eggebrecht, Hans Heinrich. "Zum Wort-Ton-Verhältnis in der *Musica poetica* von J. A. Herbst," in *Gesellschaft für Musikforschung, Bericht über den internationalen musikwissenschaftlichen Kongress Hamburg 1956*. Kassel: Bärenreiter, 1957. (77-80.)

Farmer, Henry George. *A History of Music in Scotland*. London: Hinrichson, 1947.

Federhofer, Helmut. "Die Figurenlehre nach Christoph Bernhard und die Dissonanzbehandlung in Werken von Heinrich Schütz," in *Gesellschaft der Musikforschung Bericht über den internationalen musikwissenschaftlichen Kongress Bamberg 1953*. Kassel: Bärenreiter, 1953. (132-135.)

Feldman, Fritz. "Mattheson und die Rhetorik," in *Gesellschaft für Musikforschung Bericht über den internationalen musikwissenschaftlichen Kongress Hamburg 1956*. Kassel: Bärenreiter, 1957. (99-103.)

Fiske, R. *English Theatre Music in the Eighteenth Century*. London: Oxford University Press, 1973.

Flaherty, M. G. "Lessing and Opera: A Re-evaluation," *The Germanic Review*, XLIV (1969), 95-109.

__________. *Opera and Incipient Romantic Aesthetics in Germany*. Cleveland: Case Western University Press, 1973.

__________. *Opera in the Development of German Critical Thought*. Princeton: Princeton University Press, 1978.

Fletcher, Harris Francis. The Intellectual Development of John Milton. Urbana: University of Illinoins Press, 1961.

__________. Milton's Rabbinical Readings. Urbana: University of Illinois Press, 1930.

__________. Milton's Semitic Studies. New York: Gordian Press, 1926.

Forchert, Arno. "Französische Autoren in den Schriften Johann Matthesons," in Festschrift Heinz Becker. Laaber: Laaber Verlag, 1982, 383-391.

Forsyth, Cecil. Music and Nationalism. A Study of English Opera. London: Macmillan, 1911.

Freier, Hans. Kritische Poetik. Legitimation und Kritik der Poesie in "Gottscheds Dichtkunst". Stuttgart: J. B. Metzler, 1973.

Fuchs, Peter. "Holste," in Neue deutsche Biographie, Vol. 9, 548-550. Berlin: Duncker und Humblot, 1971.

Gaede, Friedrich. Humanismus-Barock-Aufklärung: Geschichte vom 16. bis zum 18. Jahrhundert. Bern: Francke, 1971.

Gallaway, Francis. Reason, Rule, and Revolt in English Classicism. New York: Scribner's Sons, 1940.

Gelobter, Hanna. "Le Spectateur" von Pierre Marivaux und die englischen moralistischen Wochenschriften. Frankfurt: n.p., 1936.

Gilmore, Thomas B., Jr. Early Eighteenth-Century Essays on Taste. Delmar, New York: Scholars' Facsimiles and Reprints, 1972.

Goldschmidt, Hugo. Die Musikästhetik des 18. Jahrhunderts. Zurich and Leipzig: Rascher, 1915.

Graham, Walter. The Beginnings of English Literary Periodicals. New York: Oxford University Press, 1926.

__________. English Literary Periodicals. New York: Thomas Nelson and Sons, 1930.

Grant, Kerry S. Dr. Burney as Critic and Historian of Music. Ann Arbor: UMI Reseach Press, 1983.

Gurr, J. E. "Rationalism," in The New Catholic Encyclopedia. New York: McGraw-Hill, 1967. (Vol. 12, 90-93.)

Haar, James. "Musica Mundana: Variations on a Pythagorian Theme." Unpubl. Ph.D. dissertation. Harvard University, 1961.

Haase, Rudolf. Geschichte des Harmonikalen Pythagorismus. Vienna: Lafite, 1969.

Hagstrom, E. The Sister Arts. Chicago: University of Chicago Press, 1958.

Halevy, M. P. "Boileau-Despreaux," in The New Catholic Encyclopedia. New York: McGraw-Hill, 1967. (Vol.2, 639-640.)

Hampson, Norman. A Cultural History of the Enlightenment. New York: Pantheon Books, 1968.

Hanford, James Holly. A Milton Handbook. New York: F. S. Crofts, 1933.

Harris, Ellen. "An American Offers Advice to Handel," in American Choral Review, XXVII (1985), 55-62.

Haslinger, Adolf. Epische Formen im höfischen Barockroman. Munich: W. Finck, 1970.

Hauser, Arnold. Sozialgeschichte der Kunst und Literatur. Munich: Beck, 1953.

Hayes, Gerald R. "Charles Butler and the Music of the Bees," Musical Times, XLVI (1925), 512-515.

Hettner, Hermann. Geschichte der deutschen Literatur im achtzehnten Jahrhundert. Leipzig: Paul List, 1929.

__________. Geschichte der englischen Literatur. Fifth edition. Braunschweig: Friedrich Vieweg, 1894.

Hipple, Walter John, Jr. The Beautiful, the Sublime, and

the Picturesque in Eighteenth-Century British Aesthetic Theory. Carbondale, Illinois: Southern Illinois University Press, 1957.

Honour, Hugh. Neo-Classicism. London: Penguin, 1968.

Hosler, Bellamy. Changing Aesthetic Views of Instrumental Music in 18th-Century Germany. Ann Arbor: UMI Reseach Press, 1981.

Hüschen, Heinrich. "Der Polyhistor Gerhard Johann Vossius (1577-1649) als Musikschriftsteller," in Festschrift für Walter Wiora. Kassel: Bärenreiter, 1967.

Johnson, David. Music and Society in Lowland Scotland in the Eighteenth Century. London: Oxford University Press, 1972.

Johnson, J. W. The Formation of English Neo-Classical Thought. Princeton: Princeton University Press, 1967.

Kassler, Jamie Croy. The Science of Music in Britain, 1714-1830. A Catalogue of Writings, Lectures and Inventions. New York: Garland Publishing, 1979.

Keller, H. "Johann Adolf Scheibe und Johann Sebastian Bach," in Musik und Verlag: Karl Vötterle zum 65. Geburtstag. Kassel: Bärenreiter, 1968.

Ker, W. P., ed. Essays of John Dryden. Oxford: Oxford University Press, 1926.

Kidson, Frank. "Alexander Malcolm in America," Music and Letters, XXXIII (1952), 226-231.

Kivy, Peter. The Seventh Sense: A Study of Francis Hutcheson's Aesthetics and its Influence in Eighteenth-Century Britain. New York: Burt Franklin, 1976.

Klein, Hannelore. There is no Disputing about Taste. Untersuchungen zum englischen Geschmacksbegriff im achtzehnten Jahrhundert. Münster: Aschendorf, 1967.

Knapp, J. Merrill. "A Forgotten Chapter in English Eighteenth-Century Opera," Music and Letters, XLIII (1962), 4-16.

Köster, Albert. *Die deutsche Literatur der Aufklärungszeit*. Heidelberg: Carl Winter, 1925.

Kross, Siegfried. "Mattheson und Gottsched," in *New Mattheson Studies*. Ed. by George Buelow and Hans Joachim Marx. New York: Cambridge University Press, 1983.

Larsen, Jens Peter. "Some Observations on the Development and Characteristics of Vienna Classical Instrumental Music," *Studia Musicologica*, 9 (1967), 136.

Laure, Margaret. "Addison," in *New Grove's Dictionary*, I, 104.

Le Huray, Peter, and James Day, eds. *Music and Aesthetics in the Eighteenth and Early-Nineteenth Centuries*. Cambridge: Cambridge University Press.

Lenneberg, Hans. "Johann Mattheson on Affect and Rhetoric in Music," *Journal of Music Theory*, II (1958), 47-84; 193-236.

Lewis, Christopher. "Incipient Tonal Thought in Seventeenth-Century English Theory," *Studies in Music from Western Ontario*, 6 (1981), 24-46.

Lewis, C. S. "Addison," in *Eighteenth-Century English Literature: Modern Essays in Criticism*. Ed. by James Clifford. New York: Oxford University Press, 1959.

Lipking, Lawrence. *The Ordering of the Arts in Eighteenth-Century England*. Princeton: Princeton University Press, 1970.

Loemker, Leroy E. *Struggle for Synthesis--The Seventeenth-Century Background of Leibniz's Synthesis of Order and Freedom*. Cambridge: Harvard University Press, 1972.

Lovejoy, Arthur O. *Essays in the History of Ideas*. Baltimore: Johns Hopkins Press, 1948.

Lowens, Irving. "*The Touch-Stone* (1728): A Neglected View of London Opera," in *Musical Quarterly*, XLV (1959), 325-342.

MacKerness, E. D. A Social History of Music. London: Rutledge & Paul, 1964.

Maesch, Lavahn. "A Survey of Musical Development in England from 1627 to 1660." Unpubl. master's thesis. University of Rochester, 1936.

Mann, Alfred, ed. J. J. Fux: Gradus ad Parnassum. Kassel and Graz: Bärenreiter, 1967.

Manuel, Frank, ed. The Enlightenment. Englewood Cliffs, N.J.: Prentice-Hall, 1965.

Martin, Dennis R. The Operas and Operatic Style of John Frederick Lampe. Detroit: Detroit Monographs in Musicology, Number 8, 1985.

Masson, David. The Life of John Milton. London: Macmillan, 1875.

Middleton, Lydia Miller. "Pepusch," in DNB, XV, 199-210.

Miller, Gertrude. "Tonal Materials in Seventeenth-Century English Theorists." Unpubl. Ph.D dissertation. University of Rochester, 1960.

Monk, Samuel K. The Sublime. Ann Arbor: University of Michigan Press, 1960.

Monro, D. B. The Modes of Ancient Greek Music. Oxford: Clarendon Press, 1894.

Nagel, Willibald. Geschichte der Musik in England. Strasbourg: K. J. Trübner, 1897.

Neubecker, Annemarie Jeanette. Altgriechische Musik. Darmstadt: Wissenschaftliche Buchgesellschaft, 1977.

Nivelle, Armand. Kunst- und Dichtungs-Theorien zwischen Aufklärung und Klassik. Berlin: de Gruyter, 1960.

Oppel, H. Englisch-deutsche Literaturbeziehungen. Berlin: de Gruyter, 1971.

Otten, Robert M. Joseph Addison. Boston: Twayne, 1982.

Pfrogner, Hermann. Musik: Geschichte ihrer Bedeutung. Munich: Karl Alber, 1954.

Prince, F. T. The Italian Element in Milton's Verse. Oxford: Clarendon Press, 1954.

Pruett, James. "Charles Butler --Musician, Grammarian, Apiarist," Musical Quarterly, XLIX (1963), 498-509.

Randall, Jane. The Origins of the Scottish Enlightenment. London: Macmillan, 1978.

Raynor, Henry. Music in England. London: R. Hale, 1980.

Ruff, Lillian. "The 17th-Century English Music Theorists." Unpubl. Ph.D. dissertation. University of Nottingham, 1962.

Saisselin, Rémy G. The Rule of Reason and the Ruses of the Heart. A Philosophical Dictionary of Classical French Criticism, Critics, and Aesthetic Issues. Cleveland: Case Western Reserve University Press, 1970.

__________. Taste in Eighteenth-Century France. Critical Reflections on the Origin of Aesthetics; or An Apology for Amateurs. Syracuse: Syracuse University Press, 1965.

Saurat, Denis. Milton: Man and Thinker. New York: Dial, 1925.

Scharlau, Ulf. Athanasius Kircher (1601-1680) als Musikschriftsteller. Marburg: n.p., 1969.

Schmitz, Arnold. "Die oratorische Kunst J. S. Bachs--Grundfragen und Grundlagen," in Gesellschaft für Musikforschung Kongress Bericht Lüneburg. Kassel: Bärenreiter, 1950, 33-49.

Schneider, Herbert. "Mattheson und die französische Musik," in New Mattheson Studies, ed. by George Buelow and Hans Joachim Marx. Cambridge: Cambridge University Press, 1983, 425-442.

Scholes, Percy. The Oxford Companion to Music. London: Oxford University Press, 1950.

Schoolfield, George. _The Figure of the Musician in German Literature_. Chapel Hill: University of North Carolina Press, 1956.

Schueller, Herbert M. "Literature and Music as Sister Arts: An Aspect of Aesthetic Theory in Eighteenth-Century Britain," _Philological Quarterly_, XXVI (1947), 195.

__________. "The Quarrel of the Ancients and Moderns," _Musical Times_, 101 (1960), 313-330.

__________. "The Use and Decorum of Music as Described in British Literature, 1700 to 1780," _Journal of the History of Ideas_, XIII (1952), 73-93.

Schultze, Walter. _Die Quellen der Hamburger Oper_. Hamburg: Gerhard Stalling, 1938.

Schwann, Wilhelm Bernhard. "Die opernästhetischen Theorien der deutschen klassischen Dichter." Unpubl. Ph.D. dissertation. University of Bonn, 1928.

Scott, William Robert. _Frances Hutcheson: His Life, Teaching and Position in the History of Philosophy_. New York: Augustus M. Kelly, 1966.

Seibel, Gustav Adolph. _Das Leben des königl. polnischen und kurfürstl. Sächs. Hofkapellmeisters Johann David Heinichen_. Leipzig: Breitkopf & Härtel, 1913.

Serauky, Walter. _Die musikalische Nachahmungsästhetik im Zeitraum von 1700 bis 1850_. Münster: Helios, 1929.

Skapski, G. J. "The Recitative in J. A. Scheibe's Literary and Musical Work." Unpubl. Ph.D. dissertation. University of Texas, 1963.

Smithers, Peter. _The Life of Joseph Addison_. Oxford: Clarendon Press, 1968.

Spaeth, Sigmund. _Milton's Knowledge of Music_. Princeton: University Library, 1913.

Spingarn, J. E., ed. _Critical Essays of the Seventeenth Century_. Oxford: Oxford University Press, 1908.

Stege, Fritz. "Die deutsche Musikkritik des 18. Jahrhunderts unter dem Einfluß der Affektenlehre," Zeitschrift für Musikwissenschaft, X (1927-1928), 23-30.

Sumner, William Leslie. The Organ: its Evolution, Principles of Construction and Use. 4th ed. London: MacDonald and Jane's, 1973.

Sutherland, James. English Literature of the Late Seventeenth Century. Oxford: Clarendon Press, 1969.

Tanner, Richard. Johann David Heinichen als dramatischer Komponist: ein Beitrag zur Geschichte der Oper. Leipzig: Breitkopf & Härtel, 1916.

Tillyard, E. M. M. Milton. New York: Dial, 1930.

Tilmouth, Michael. "Finger," in New Grove's Dictionary, 6, 565-566.

__________. "Prendcourt," in New Grove's Dictionary, 15, 214-215.

Tisch, J. H. "Milton and the German Mind in the Eighteenth Century," in Studies in the Eighteenth Century. Papers Presented at the David Nichol Smith Memorial Seminar. Canberra: Australian National University Press, 1968.

Tumarkin, Anna. "Die Überwindung der Mimesis-Lehre in der Kunsttheorie des XVIII. Jahrhunderts," in Festgabe für Samuel Singer. Tübingen: J. C. B. Mohr, 1930.

Tuveson, Ernest. The Imagination as a Means of Grace. Locke and the Aesthetics of Romanticism. Berkeley: University of California Press, 1960.

__________. "Shaftesbury and the Age of Sensibility," in Studies in Criticism and Aesthetics, 1660-1800. Essays in Honor of Samuel Holt Monk. Minneapolis: University of Minnesota Press, 1967, 73-93.

Unger, Heinz-Heinrich. Die Beziehungen zwischen Musik und Rhetorik im 16.-18. Jahrhundert. Würzburg: Konrad Triltsch, 1942.

Vivian, Percival. Campion's Works. London: Oxford University Press, 1907.

Walker, Ernest. A History of Music in England. Oxford, 1952.

Warry, J. Greek Aesthetic Theory. London, 1934. 1962.

Weisbach, Werner. Vom Geschmack und seinen Wandlungen. Bassel: Amerbach, 1947.

Weiser, Christian. Shaftesbury und das deutsche Geistesleben. Leipzig: Teubner, 1916.

Werckmeister, Willhelm. Der Stilwandel in deutscher Dichtung und Musik des 18. Jahrhunderts. Berlin: Junker & Dünnhaupt, 1936.

Wessel, Frederick T. "The Affektenlehre in the Eighteenth Century." Unpubl. Ph.D. dissertation. University of Indiana, 1967.

West, Robert H. Milton and the Angels. Athens, Georgia: University of Georgia Press, 1955.

Wilheim, Immanuel. "Johann Adolph Scheibe: German Musical Thought in Transition." Unpubl. Ph.D dissertation. University of Illinois, 1963.

Wilson, John, ed. Roger North on Music, Being a Selection from His Essays Written During the Years c.1695-1728. London: Novello, 1959.

__________. "North," in New Grove's Dictionary, 13, 286.

Winn, James Anderson. Unsuspected Eloquence: A History of the Relations between Poetry and Music. New Haven: Yale University Press, 1981.

Wöhlke, Franz. Lorenz Christoph Mizler. Würzburg: Konrad Triltsch, 1940.

Wolff, Ernest Georg. Grundlagen einer autonomen Musikästhetik. Leipzig: Heitz, 1934.

Woodfill, Walter. Musicians in English Society from Elizabeth to Charles I. Princeton: Princeton University Press, 1953.

Young, Percy. *A History of British Music*. New York: Norton, 1967.

Zart, G. *Einfluss der englischen Philosophen seit Bacon auf die deutsche Philosophie des 18. Jahrhunderts*. Berlin: Ferdinand Dümmler, 1881.

Ziebler, Karl. "Zur Ästhetik der Lehre von den musikalischen Redefiguren im 18. Jahrhundert," *Zeitschrift für Musikwissenschaft*, XV (1932-1933), 289-301.

INDEX